P9-CAM-180

FRIEDRICH SCHILLER

Born in 1759, Johann Christoph Friedrich von Schiller wrote his first play, *The Robbers* (staged: 1782), while he was a regimental surgeon at the military academy in Württemberg. Fleeing from the Duke of Württemberg's displeasure at the play, he accepted a contract from the National Theatre at Mannheim, where he wrote *Fiesco* and *Intrigue and Love* (both staged: 1784) and where his blank verse drama, *Don Carlos*, was first performed (1787). Most of his subsequent plays were staged at the Court Theatre in Weimar, under the direction of his fellow-dramatist and poet, Goethe. These included *Egmont* (1796), for which Beethoven wrote an overture and incidental music, the *Wallenstein* trilogy (1798-99), *Mary Stuart* (1800) and *William Tell* (1804). He was professor of history at Jena from 1789 to 1791 and settled in Weimar in 1799, where he collaborated with Goethe in running the theatre until his death in 1805.

JEREMY SAMS

Starting out as a piano accompanist, Sams has since worked extensively as a musical director, composer, translator and director for theatre, opera and television. His translations include Anouilh's *The Rehearsal* and *Becket* in the West End, Molière's *The Miser* and Cocteau's *Les Parents Terribles* for the Royal National Theatre, *La Cendrillon* for Welsh National Opera and *Figaro's Wedding* and *The Magic Flute* for English National Opera. He has directed plays for Greenwich Theatre, the Nottingham Playhouse and the West Yorkshire Playhouse, and composed scores for *The Wind in the Willows* and *Arcadia* at the Royal National Theatre and for *Talking Heads* and *The Importance of Being Earnest* in the West End. He also directed his own adaptation of *Wild Oats* for the National and the British premiere of Stephen Sondheim's *Passion* in the West End.

Other Classics in Translation

Anton Chekhov
THE SEAGULL
UNCLE VANYA
tr. Pam Gems

Anton Chekhov
THREE SISTERS
tr. Stephen Mulrine

Jean Cocteau
LES PARENTS TERRIBLES
(INDISCRETIONS)
tr. Jeremy Sams

Corneille
THE ILLUSION
tr. Tony Kushner

Euripides
MEDEA
*tr. Kenneth McLeish &
Frederic Raphael*

Goethe
FAUST
tr. Howard Brenton

Henrik Ibsen
A DOLL'S HOUSE
HEDDA GABLER
PEER GYNT
tr. Kenneth McLeish

Henrik Ibsen
AN ENEMY OF THE
PEOPLE
tr. Arthur Miller

Federico Garcia Lorca
BLOOD WEDDING &
YERMA
*tr. Langston Hughes & WS
Mervin*

Molière
THE HYPOCHONDRIAC
tr. Martin Sorrell

Alfred de Musset
FANTASIO AND OTHER
PLAYS
various translators

Edmond Rostand
CYRANO DE BERGERAC
tr. Anthony Burgess

Seneca
THYESTES
tr. Caryl Churchill

August Strindberg
MISS JULIE
tr. Kenneth McLeish

FRIEDRICH SCHILLER

MARY STUART

translated by
JEREMY SAMS

ROYAL NATIONAL THEATRE
London

NICK HERN BOOKS
London

Mary Stuart first published in this edition in Great Britain in 1996 as a paperback original jointly by the Royal National Theatre, London and Nick Hern Books Ltd, 14 Larden Road, London W3 7ST

Translation © Jeremy Sams 1996
Introduction copyright © Nick Hern Books Ltd 1996

Jeremy Sams has asserted his moral right to be identified as the translator of this work

Front cover: Elizabeth I (unknown artist) and Mary Queen of Scots (unknown artist), courtesy National Portrait Gallery

Typeset by Country Setting, Woodchurch, Kent TN26 3TB
Printed and bound by Cox and Wyman Ltd, Reading, Berks

A CIP catalogue record for this book is available from the British Library

ISBN 1 85459 294 7

CAUTION

All rights whatsoever in this play are stricly reserved. Requests to reproduce the text in whole or in part should be addressed to the publisher.

Amateur Performing Rights: applications for performance by amateurs throughout the world (except in the United States of America and Canada) should be addressed to Nick Hern Books, 14 Larden Road, London W3 7ST (*fax* 0181 746-2006).

Professional Performing Rights: Applications for performance in any medium and in any language by professionals throughout the world (and for stock and amateur performance in the United States of America and Canada) should be addressed to Jeremy Sams's agent, Michael Imison Playwrights Ltd, 28 Almeida Street, London N1 1TD.

No performance may take place unless a licence has been obtained and application should be made before rehearsals begin.

Introduction

Eighteenth-Century German Drama and *Sturm und Drang*

Germany was later than most western European countries in developing a native professional theatre. It was not until 1767 (with Lessing's *Minna von Barnhelm*) that a major play with German characters and a German setting was written. The subsequent drama of the 1770s was dominated by the *Sturm und Drang* (literally Storm and Stress) movement. Enlightenment classicism was rejected in favour of a more epic, individualistic drama which acknowledged a great debt to the plays of Shakespeare, which at that time were being translated into German. Specifically and consciously German, the *Sturm und Drang* plays appealed to a developing sense of nationhood amongst the German states. The plays focused on the individual hero and in particular on the heroic character under severe stress: plots include patricide, incest and violent suffering. This is drama that is less concerned with the more classical predilection for the unpredictable and inexorable processes of fate than with the imposing romanticism of the individual. *Sturm und Drang* plays often involved a degree of social criticism, especially of the class system. The plays of Lenz and Goethe typify the movement, and the early work of Schiller, although written in the 1780s, reveals an immense debt to the drama of the previous decade.

Friedrich Schiller (1759–1805)

Schiller's first play, *The Robbers*, was written in 1781 while he was a disillusioned recruit in the military academy at Württemberg. The other two plays counted as Schiller's *Sturm und Drang* plays, *The Conspiracy of Fiesco at Genoa* (1781-2) and *Intrigue and Love* (1782-3), were written while he was the house dramatist at Mannheim. All bear witness to his youthful idealism and reveal an indebtedness to Shakespeare.

However, *Intrigue and Love* marks Schiller's departure from *Sturm und Drang* values and a movement towards a more classical idiom. This period has come to be termed the 'Weimar Style', a distinctive mixture of the classical and the romantic. The drama displays classical influences, not only on subject matter but on form and structure (Goethe's *Iphigenia in Tauris* dates from this time). *Don Carlos* was written over a period of several years during the 1780s. Schiller arrived in Weimar in 1787; the next few years of his life were devoted to the study of history, philosophy and aesthetics. He was appointed professor of history at Jena University in 1789. He returned to drama with his trilogy on Wallenstein (all 1799). In 1800 he wrote *Mary Stuart* which he described as a 'romantic tragedy'. Schiller's final years were spent at Weimar. where he found a friend and collaborator in Goethe and it was during this period that he produced much of his best work: *The Maid of Orleans* (1801), the 1803 play, *The Bride of Messina*, a conscious reworking of Greek tragedy, and his final completed play, *Wilhelm Tell* in 1804.

Themes in *Mary Stuart*

Mary Stuart centres on the last days of Mary Queen of Scots and her troubled relationship with her cousin, Elizabeth I of England. Mary was held prisoner in a series of castles over a period of nineteen years, and although the play depicts a meeting between them, in reality the queens did not meet. The dramatic central meeting in the park of Fotheringay Castle offers Schiller the ideal opportunity to demonstrate the personal differences between the sensual, passionate Mary and the more political and pragmatic Elizabeth. Indeed, the play centres on the contrast between Mary's 'grief... gentleness... and... patience in adversity' (I vi) and Elizabeth, the 'vile, lubricious, double-dealing queen' (II vi). Where Mary inspires a devotion bordering on idolatry among her entourage, Elizabeth's court is a hotbed of corruption, double-dealing, paranoia and anxiety. It is this contrast, the pursuit of the emotional versus the political, which characterises much of the action of the play.

At Westminster, what is of consequence is seeming. The necessity of monarchy for Elizabeth is the relationship between image and truth:

> I have to seem to be responsible and yet maintain the
> appearance of detatchment. (II v).

Guilt and responsibility are significant themes within the framework of the play. Mary's compelling complexity is rooted in her own perception of her past crimes, and she is depicted as being motivated, at least in part, by guilt. Elizabeth is not the sole enemy of Mary; her own past informs against her. Mary is erroneous in claiming to Mortimer that her right to the English throne is 'The only cause of all my suffering' (I vi). To her mind, only Catholic communion will release her from the murder of Darnley, and when Melville offers her this opportunity in Act V she is able to make peace with her conscience in a way that remains impossible for Elizabeth. Indeed, Mary achieves in her death the release and freedom that Elizabeth craves. The play draws parallels between their states of confinement: while Mary's imprisonment is physical, Elizabeth's is metaphysical. Elizabeth is portrayed as a character profoundly disillusioned with the processes of monarchy, and the play ends on a stark depiction of her isolation.

The contrast between Mary and Elizabeth is mirrored in the difference between Mortimer and Leicester. The play emphasises the freeing of Mortimer in his suicide while Leicester finds himself ensnared by his own politicking:

> She has gone – her soul quite transfigured – and I'm left here, damned to despair. (V i)

Whilst often historically accurate, *Mary Stuart* concertinas actual historical events: for example, the length of Mary's detention and Elizabeth's extrication from the Alençon marriage. However, Schiller succeeds in clearly delineating the problems of religion in Elizabethan England, charting the conflicts between Catholic and Protestant Churches that were such central issues to the recent and fragile Protestant monarchy.

Schiller's Dramatic Theory

Mary Stuart demonstrates Schiller's preoccupation with classical form while retaining the more immediately personal and romantic strains of *Sturm und Drang*. Schiller's theory of tragedy holds up the modern as distinct from the ancient Greek, a theory expounded in his essay *On Naive and Sentimental Poetry* (1797). Here Schiller stresses the fact that the modern writer detects a harmony in nature which is lacking in the self: this is termed the 'Sentimental'. In contrast, the ancient Greek dramatist was unaware of any difference between the self and nature and is defined as 'Naive'. Developing this idea further, Schiller applied it to the idea of the Sublime. The distinction drawn between Beauty and the Sublime is defined by Schiller in his essay *On the Sublime*:

Beauty offers no challenge to the Reason while the Sublime makes us aware of disharmony within ourselves.

It is the Sublime which Schiller seeks to demonstrate in his tragedies. His essay, *On the Pathetic* suggests that the purpose of tragedy is to move the audience to sympathy rather than offer moral example:

> the tragic hero must first of all establish himself as a being capable of feeling before we will honour him as one capable of Reason and believe in his strength of soul.

Suffering is a means of demonstrating the hero's Sublimity, either active or passive. It is Schiller's conception of active Sublimity which informs *Mary Stuart*; the protagonist's suffering is brought about by repentance of a past deed. It is this repentance which Schiller conceives of as particularly relevant to tragic drama.

Schiller's drama privileges emotion and contemporary notions of dramatic structure: the theatrical genre was developed by Schiller to include the psychological and intimate personal state of the protagonist in a manner more usually connected with the novel.

Performance History

In 1784, a theatre was constructed in Weimar to replace the earlier amateur court theatre which had been housed within the palace of the Duchess Anna Amalia. The old theatre had been run by Goethe with a group of courtiers to produce plays for royal occasions. This theatre admitted courtiers free of charge, but members of the public had to pay.

The new Court Theatre (Hoftheater) boasted its own professional company, and it was to this theatre that Goethe was appointed as Artistic Director in 1791. Together, Goethe and Schiller worked to create their vision of a theatre characterised as much by high theatricality as literary and intellectual endeavour. The repertory included (among others) plays by Shakespeare, Calderon, Lessing and Voltaire as well as by Goethe and Schiller themselves. The theatre was renovated in 1798 in a neo-clasical style, with pillars painted to resemble antique marble. The first performance of *Maria Stuart* took place in this building on 14 June 1800.

The recent history of the play in Britain includes productions of Stephen Spender's translation at the London Old Vic in 1958 and 1960. The Citizens' Theatre in Glasgow presented the play in a translation by Robert David MacDonald in 1988, and Greenwich Theatre mounted a production of the same translation in 1989 with Fiona Shaw and Paola Dionisotti as Mary and Elizabeth.

Gaynor Macfarlane

This new version of Schiller's *Mary Stuart* by Jeremy Sams was first staged at the Royal National Theatre, London. First preview was on 15 March, 1996 and press night on 21 March 1996. The cast was as follows:

HANNA KENNEDY	Gillian Barge
PAULET	Patrick Godfrey
MARY STUART	Isabelle Huppert
MORTIMER	Ben Miles
BURLEIGH	Paul Jesson
DAVISON	Colin Hurley
KENT	Seymour Matthews
ELIZABETH I	Anna Massey
AUBESPINE	Christopher Campbell
BELLIEVRE	Collin Johnson
TALBOT	James Grout
LEICESTER	Tim Pigott-Smith
O'KELLY	Will Keen
MELVILLE	Osmund Bullock
BURGOYNE	Randal Herley
SHERIFF	Jonathan Deverell
OFFICER	Jean Benoit-Blanc
OFFICER	James Nickerson
ROSAMUND	Cathy French
ALICE	Naomi Capron

The music is played live by
Paul Higgs (*music director/keyboards*)
Deborah Boyes (*oboe*)
Paul Kellett (*cello*)

Director   Howard Davies
Designer   William Dudley
Lighting   David Hersey
Music   Jason Carr
Fight   William Hobbs
Company Voice Work   Patsy Rodenburg
Sound   Jonathan Suffolk

MARY STUART

Cast of Characters

HANNA KENNEDY
PAULET
DRURY
MARY STUART
MORTIMER
BURLEIGH
DAVISON
KENT
ELIZABETH I
AUBESPINE
BELLIEVRE
TALBOT
LEICESTER
O'KELLY
OFFICER
PAGE
MELVILLE
BURGOYNE
ALICE
ROSAMUND
SHERIFF

and further nobles, soldiers, guards, etc.

Act One Scene One

Fotheringay Castle.

HANNA KENNEDY, MARY*'s nurse, is tussling with* PAULET, *who is trying to force open a cupboard.* DRURY, *his assistant, is helping with a crowbar.*

KENNEDY. How dare you! The impudence! Get away from here. This is private . . .

PAULET. How did you come by this jewel? Thrown down from your window! Trying to bribe the gardeners, were we? Women's tricks. Despite our vigilance and all our careful searches – and well, well, here's more trumpery, more gewgaws and knickknacks. And I wonder what else . . .

KENNEDY. Have you no respect? These are my lady's deepest secrets.

PAULET. Good. Just what we're looking for.

KENNEDY. Just idle pastimes; to while away the misery of prison.

PAULET. The devil's found work for her hands – I see.

KENNEDY. These are in French, so you might not . . .

PAULET. Worse and worse. The language of our enemy.

KENNEDY. Drafts of letters to the Queen of England.

PAULET. I'll make sure she gets them. Hello, what's this? A royal crown, all carbuncled with jewels, and crawling with the fleur-de-lys of France. I think we'll keep that – put it with the rest.

Exit DRURY.

KENNEDY. I beg you sir, spare us that. The last remaining vestiges of majesty. She loves to gaze on them and to remember.

PAULET. They're in safe hands – and will doubtless be returned to you in time.

KENNEDY. Who'd guess from these bare walls, a queen
    dwelt here?
  Where is the canopy above her throne?
  Her dainty feet are chafed and bleeding from
  This carpeting of ash and dirt and stone.
  You serve our food on tin plate . . .

PAULET. She thought that good enough for Lord Darnley while
  she and her paramour slobbered over gold.

KENNEDY. . . . and no mirrors . . .

PAULET. Vanity. The more she sees her face, the more she hopes
  and dreams and plots.

KENNEDY. No books to entertain her.

PAULET. We left her the Bible – for a little self-improvement.

KENNEDY. You even took away her guitar.

PAULET. I think I was doing everyone a favour there!

KENNEDY. She was queen in her cradle, brought up in luxury
  and ease. It's hard enough to strip her of her power, but must
  you also sheer her of the little she possesses?

PAULET. Anything which distracts her from her proper penitence
  is wrong and merest vanity. An earthly life like hers, of
  opulence and lust should be atoned in poverty and prayer.

KENNEDY. If she offended in her youth, may God condemn her
  and may her heart do penance. But there's no-one here in
  England that can judge her.

PAULET. She must be judged wherever she has sinned.

KENNEDY. But in prison here, what crime can she commit?

PAULET. Oh yes?
    Although immured and guarded and in chains,
  She somehow still insinuates her arm
  Through prison bars and castle walls; to beckon,
  To lure and to pollute our English youth;
  To snap her fingers and produce the spark
  To summon up the flames of Civil War.
  She arms assassins, Babington and Parry
  And from this cell she bids them kill the Queen.
  The worst crime in the world. Did these stone walls
  Prevent her from ensnaring Norfolk's heart?
  When his head fell, there fell the best of England.

And all for her . . .
     Did his example hold the others back?
No, thousands of fanatics, hot for her,
Who'd die for her. And have. And will. The traffic of
The scaffold will not stop till she is on it.

KENNEDY. She came here as a suppliant, a refugee
To ask the young Queen's help, and here it is . . . This.
Arrested, thrown in jail, forced to watch her youth and beauty
fade. And now, after all that, dragged like a common criminal
before the court accused of God knows what.

PAULET. She came into this country as a murderess. Unthroned
and driven out of Scotland, toppled from the throne that she'd
defiled. All she wanted was the overthrow of England, to make
us Catholics, to sell us to the French. She could have renounced
her claims on England and sprung open these prison gates with
the twitch of a quill. But no. She wanted to be here. A victim. A
mistreated angel. A cause. Why? Because she has put her trust
in spies and in double agents and intriguers. And thus she spins
her evil web and tries to conquer England from this cell.

KENNEDY. Haven't we suffered enough without your sneers?
Any dreams she may have had lie buried here. Buried alive. Not
a voice of comfort, nor of home has penetrated these walls. Not
a single human face, save that of our jailers, our persecutors.

PAULET. How do I know that these walls, this floor, aren't
undermined. That treason doesn't seep through the flagstones,
like some vile miasma. This is a wretched job. To guard this
double-dealing, rabble-rousing monster. Every night I stalk the
castle like a soul in purgatory. Sleep's impossible, so I check
and double check the locks and bolts and terrorise the guards.
And every dawn is as cold and dank as my fear, that today . . .
And so I pray that it should end, end soon. I'd rather guard the
legions of the damned at the gates of Hell than watch over this
slippery queen.

KENNEDY. She's here.

PAULET. Yes. Her 'saviour' in her hand. And God knows what
ambition in her heart.

Act One Scene Two

Enter MARY *in a veil, a crucifix in her hand.*

KENNEDY. Your Majesty. Such pointless cruelty, tyranny. Shame on shame and more humiliation all poured on your sweet Majesty's sweet head.

MARY. Hanna, pull yourself together. What's been happening?

KENNEDY. Look, they broke into your desk. They found our hidden secrets. Your documents, your wedding jewels from France, the last vestiges of royalty all defiled.

MARY. It takes more than gold and jewels to make a Queen. These men can treat us basely but not debase us. I've learned a lot in England – many things – but mostly how to swallow pain. Anyway, sir, you have merely done by force what I intended by my free will. So thanks. Among the pages is a letter to my sister, Queen of England. Please give me your word that you'll deliver it directly and in person, and not, I pray, to Lord Burleigh, or his kind.

PAULET. I'll do what I consider best.

MARY. I beg her, in this letter, for a favour. A great favour. The privilege of an audience with her. The woman I've never met. I was tried by men, men I could not recognise and who could not know my heart. Elizabeth is of my stock, my rank, my sex. I can only open up my heart to an equal, a sister, a fellow queen. A woman.

PAULET. You've not hitherto been noticeably shy of men. And men not worthy of your attention, let alone your affection.

MARY. And I've asked a second favour – one that only inhumanity could refuse. For many years I've lived without the comfort of the church, and of the holy sacraments. She who robbed me of my freedom, and my crown, and has threatened to rob me of my life, can hardly slam the gates of Heaven in my face.

PAULET. The prison chaplain, if you wish, will visit you.

MARY. I don't want chaplains. I demand a priest of my own church. The pain of prison has long been gnawing at me. I feel it, like a cancer, and I know my days are numbered. And like a dying woman, I wish to order my affairs.

PAULET. Excellent. And quite proper that you should. If I can help . . .

MARY. I'm sure you will. For death is always long about its
    business, perhaps a secret hand might speed it up. No. I wish to
    make my will and properly dispose of what is mine.

PAULET. You are quite free. The Queen of England would never
    conspire to rob you of what is yours.

He turns to go.

MARY. Again you turn to leave me here in darkness
    In double darkness. Dreadful. Rotting here
    In agony and fear and, worst of all,
    In ignorance. So tell me . . .
        A month ago it was that forty men,
    Commissioners or some such, burst inside
    My chambers, dragged me off to some ramshackle
    Courtroom. Ludicrous. Not even built.
    And then, denied the help of an attorney,
    I stood, confused, half stunned, compelled to listen
    To charge and countercharge in subtle rhetoric.
    Vicious allegations. Which I tried to
    Refute – but was I making any sense?
    They came like ghosts that night. And so they went.
    And since that day I've tried to read the verdict
    In your eyes. My innocence or your hate.
    Which has prevailed? No, tell me. I must know.
        What should I do?

PAULET. You should make your peace with Heaven.

MARY. I trust that Heaven will be merciful, sir. Meanwhile I long
    for justice here on earth.

PAULET. Justice will be done, have no fear of that.

MARY. Is my case decided?

PAULET. I don't know.

MARY. Am I condemned?

PALLET. I really know nothing, my lady.

MARY. They do things quickly here. Will my executioner steal in
    at night, like my judges did?

PAULET. It's better to assume that he will. Then at least he'll find
    you at peace.

MARY. But what would England's Queen dare to do, or dare to be
    seen to have done?

PAULET. Those who rule England have nothing to fear but their consciences and Parliament. That which has been justly decreed will be carried out quite openly with the utmost force.

Act One Scene Three

Enter MORTIMER, *who studiously ignores the Queen. To* PAULET:

MORTIMER. Uncle, you're wanted.

Exit.

MARY. One last request. Let me deal with you. At least I can honour your years – but your arrogant nephew. Spare me his rudeness, his disdain.

PAULET. The more he disgusts you, the more I value him. He's experienced, he's seen the world. Paris, Rheims. And he came home an Englishman. My lady, he's immune to your black arts. Farewell.

Exit.

Act One Scene Four

KENNEDY. How dare he speak to you like that?

MARY (*lost in reflection*). In our glory days we listened far too willingly to flatterers. So it's only fair, isn't it Hanna? that we now get the rough edge of men's tongues, having enjoyed the smooth. It's all a matter of balance.

KENNEDY. This is new – you used to comfort *me*, and laugh it all away. And I would scold you for your flippancy – not your melancholy. What is it?

MARY. The bloody spectre of King Darnley, rising, stiff and bristling from the tomb. And he'll never let me know any peace – never. Not until I'm mad.

KENNEDY. Your majesty . . .

MARY. It was on this very day. You see, I'm good at dates. Every year I mark the day with penitence and fasting.

KENNEDY. Lay his ghost to rest. Years of remorse. The church forgives every sin and yours is long since dead and buried.

MARY. The grave's but lightly covered. My murdered husband's ghost howls for revenge – and needs more than a server's tinkly bell or a priest's right hand to send it back to Hell.

KENNEDY. You didn't murder him. Others did.

MARY. I knew. And did nothing to prevent it. I spun the web which caught him.

KENNEDY. You were a child. Your tender years absolve your guilt.

MARY. Tender, yes. They were. Bruised now by the weight of shame.

KENNEDY. You were driven to it. By bloody slander; by his impudence and arrogance. Your love *made* him. Plucked him from obscurity, to your bed and to the throne. You gave him your royal crown and your royal self. Your love created him, he was its masterpiece. And yet he destroyed all that. Insulted you, suspected you, and slandered you. Your creation thought he was your King. And took your favourite – Rizzio – and had him butchered before your very eyes. That bloody deed was bloodily avenged.

MARY. My bloody revenge has haunted me – most bloodily – since. Hanna, this is cold comfort.

KENNEDY. The 'you' who let the deed be done, is not you now, no part of you. You were blinded by love-madness, your seducer, vile Bothwell had quite bewitched your senses. His arrogance, his manhood had overthrown you – and then he used magic potions and black arts to confuse your mind and boil your blood.

MARY. His 'magic' was nothing more than his maleness. His rude strength . . . and my weakness.

KENNEDY. You wouldn't listen to your women, to your nurse, you turned your back on decency. Your cheeks, once damasked with a maiden's blush, burned and pulsed with rank desire. You were possessed. Lust, like man's lust, ripped away your

mystery. You stood on display, impassioned, unashamed. And
then. Then the black history begins. You let him wield the royal
sword of Scotland – and flaunt it through the streets in triumph.
You surrounded your parliament, you threatened your judges,
you set up farcical assizes to let the murderer go free – and
worst of all . . . God . . .

MARY. End it. Say it. I took him as my husband. Before the holy
altar.

KENNEDY. I know you. I brought you up from a baby. I've
known you longer than you've known yourself. Your heart is
tender, open to shame. This deed blackened your life forever, it
is true. But you haven't sinned since – I stand witness of your
reformation. So make your peace with yourself. Neither
Elizabeth nor the English parliament can judge you. You are
held here by unlawful force. You can stand before this so-called
court with all the courage of your innocence.

MARY. Someone's coming.

KENNEDY. The nephew. Quick, go inside.

Act One Scene Five

MORTIMER (*enters shyly*). Leave us and watch by the door. I
must speak with the Queen.

MARY. Hanna, stay where you are.

MORTIMER. Don't be afraid, I'll show you who I am.

Hands a letter.

MARY. My God. What's this?

MORTIMER. Leave us lady. Stand guard against my uncle.

MARY. Leave us. Do what he says.

Act One Scene Six

MARY. From my uncle, the Archbishop of Rheims: 'Trust Sir Edward Mortimer who brings you this. You have no better friend in England'. Is this some sort of trick to find a friend so near, when I'd thought myself abandoned by the world. And you? The nephew of my jailer – worse than my bitterest enemy.

MORTIMER (*kneels to her*). Majesty. Forgive me. It was a mask I had to wear. It cost me dear. And yet it brought me close to you and allowed me to help you, to rescue you.

MARY. Please get up. This is too much. To soar so quickly to hope from despair. Tell me. Explain.

MORTIMER. Time's against us. My uncle will be here. And with him, a damnable man, bearing damnable news. So listen, quickly, and I'll tell you how heaven has sent you salvation.

MARY. By a miracle of its grace.

MORTIMER. Let me tell you from the beginning.

MARY. Yes.

MORTIMER. I must have been twenty or so. I'd been brought up strictly, steeped in hatred of the Church of Rome. But there was something unfathomable which drew me away from England, away from the dreary sermonising of the Puritans. I was drawn from home, through Europe to the heat of Italy. It was a time of festival. The streets were crammed with people praying and praising God as if the whole world were one vast pilgrimage sweeping on to the gates of Heaven. Leading to Rome. And I was swept along with all the rest. How can I describe it? Oh, my Queen . . .
　　　As arcs and columns followed one another,
As Rome unfolded, History and art
In holiest alliance. I stood dumb,
A silent stranger in a wonderland.
I'd never felt the force of Art before,
The church that bred me hated opulence,
And images of faith. No, we were taught
To venerate the 'disembodied word'.
So how can I describe it . . . ?
The music that rained down on me, as if
The ceilings wept, the paintings and the colours
Which welled and burst from every wall and glowed
As if the best and holiest were crowding

Round me, plucking at my senses. Saints,
And martyrs, angels, crucifixions. Then
Flagellations and pietas
A broken mother weeping for her son
The word made flesh made real . . . and then. And then
I saw the Holy Father in his glory
He held high mass and blessed the multitude.

MARY. Enough.
Don't torture me with memories of sights
And sounds I know I'll never see again
For I am miserable, imprisoned . . .

MORTIMER. . . . So was I.
But my prison gates burst open, and my soul
Soared up as if reborn to greet the day
That bright and brave new morning of my life.
Newborn . . . in beauty . . .
    Others were there. Many brave compatriots. They
befriended me and led me to your uncle, the Cardinal of Guise.

MARY. You saw him face to face? He taught me everything. My
guardian and my guide. Did he talk of me, does he still think of
me? Is he still as strong and full of life – the bedrock of the
church?

MORTIMER. Great. Very great. But not so great that he didn't
condescend to instruct me in the Faith. From the beginning to
the end of time. The doubts and prejudices of my youth were
washed away by his logic and his eloquence. So I returned to
the bosom of the church and, thanks to him, renounced my
folly.

MARY. Thousands and thousands of blessed people. All led to
salvation by him. And now one more.

MORTIMER. It was then I heard the sorry history – I could hardly
bear to hear it – of your martyrdom. And your enemy's blood
lust. And your birth and your origins. And he explained
everything, your descent from the Royal House of Tudor, your
true claim to the throne of England. That you are the lawful
Queen and not Elizabeth, that pretender, spawned in adultery,
spurned by her own father Henry, as a bastard child. That
England is your right and for that right you are wronged. And
all this kingdom belongs to you, the very kingdom that holds
you prisoner.

MARY. My right. The only source of all my misery.

MORTIMER. About this time I heard you were to be moved from
Talbot's castle to my own uncle's. And by now I'd learned to
recognise the hand of God; the Heavens were screaming at me,
save her, now, you've been chosen. My friends agreed, the
cardinal gave me his blessing.
And so I left for home, and so, as you know, I came here.
And so I came to see, no not a portrait only but
Your face. Within this castle is a precious diamond
It's not a prison but a holy shrine,
More glorious than the royal court of England.
To breathe the same air as you . . .
And they're right to bury you so deep. They are.
For all of England's youth would rise up and gigantic outrage
would devastate the land if the English could but see their true
queen.

MARY. If they could only see her with your eyes!

MORTIMER. They'd see, as I see, your grief, your gentleness,
your patience in adversity. And most of all, your Majesty.
Every adornment has been stripped from you and still they'd
see a holy queen, shot round with light and life and fire. I can't
set foot in this cell without my heart being transfixed with
longing. I have to act, and soon. Danger's growing – terrible
things are happening.

MARY. My sentence? Has it been pronounced? Tell me, quickly. I
can bear it.

MORTIMER. It has. Forty judges find you guilty. The House of
Lords, the City of London are all eager for the execution of the
sentence. Only the Queen has yet to add her name – and that's
out of policy and guile, not goodness or mercy, not that. She's
merely waiting for them to force her hand.

MARY. Lord Mortimer, you do not surprise me nor sadden me. I'd
long expected it. You see, I know my judges, and after their
misuse of me, they're hardly likely to set me free. I know their
sentence. Eternal imprisonment, revenge on my just claim, by
burying it deep in the earth.

MORTIMER. They won't stop at that. Tyranny will never do its
work by halves. As long as you're alive, then the Queen of
England's fear of you stays alive. No dungeon can be dug deep
enough. Only your death can safeguard her throne.

MARY. Would she dare to place a crowned, anointed head upon
the block?

MORTIMER. She would. And never doubt it.

MARY. . . . profane my royal title, and her own, and that of every King and Queen? Doesn't she fear the vengeance of the French?

MORTIMER. No, no. She'll make eternal peace with France, by marriage to the Duke of Anjou.

MARY. What? But the King of Spain would rise up against her.

MORTIMER. She wouldn't fear him, nor all the armies of the world, if her country were at peace within. Other queens, your Majesty, have processed from throne to scaffold. Other crowned heads have fallen. And some not long ago.

MARY. Dear Mortimer, I do not fear the scaffold, not that. There are other ways, quieter, more subtle, to silence me and my rightful claim. Before the executioner could do his work, with pomp and ceremony, a hired hand could strike me down in secret. That's what I'm afraid of. And with every cup I put to my lips a sick shudder goes through me. Is this one laced with my sister's love?

MORTIMER. No one will murder you, not in secret, not in public. No one will touch you. Listen. Everything's prepared. There are twelve of us, young and brave and high-born. Today we made our final oath, received the sacrament upon it – that we will take you from this castle, by force if needs be. Count Aubespine, the French Ambassador knows our plans, he's offered us his help and his palace is our secret meeting place.

MARY. My God, my God. I can't breathe. My heart's pounding, not with joy, with black foreboding. Have you any idea what you are doing? The heads of Babington, of Tichburn stuck on poles on London Bridge, are they not warning enough? The countless others, thousands, whose courage led them to their deaths? And each death only made my chains the heavier. You've been seduced, fanaticised, get out while you can. The spy master, Burleigh, is sure to place a traitor in your midst, if he hasn't already. Leave this country as quickly as you can. Mary Stuart never brought anyone happiness. And never will.

MORTIMER. Those bloody heads, those thousands dead, don't frighten me. They've found their lasting glory – and happiness, for me, would be to count myself among their number.

MARY. Alas, you never will. Force can never save me, nor can stealth. Not just your uncle and his men, but the whole of

England guards my prison gates. Only the free will of Queen
Elizabeth can spring them open.

MORTIMER. You cannot hope for that.

MARY. Then there's one man in the Kingdom who can open
them.

MORTIMER. Who is it? What's his name?

MARY. The Earl . . . of Leicester.

MORTIMER. What, Leicester? Your bitterest enemy, Elizabeth's
painted darling – him?

MARY. Him. Go to him – open your heart – tell him that I sent
you. Take him this letter – my picture is in it. Take it, I've kept
it for so long hidden here. (*Her bosom.*) I'd never found a way
to send it before now, before you, my young guardian angel.

MORTIMER. Your Majesty. The Earl of Leicester – how is it that
you . . . he . . . ?

MARY. He will tell you. Trust him completely and believe me
he'll trust you. Someone's coming.

KENNEDY (*rushes on*). Sir Paulet's here, with a man from the
court.

MORTIMER. Lord Burleigh. Be strong my lady. Whatever he
says, be calm, be serene.

He exits. KENNEDY *follows.*

Act One Scene Seven

Enter BURLEIGH, *Lord Treasurer and* PAULET.

PAULET. Today you asked to hear your fate. Well here it is. My
noble Lord of Burleigh has brought this intelligence in person.
Hear it with humility and with submission.

MARY. And dignity, I trust – as befits my innocence.

BURLEIGH. I am envoy of the court.

MARY. You are more than that. You rule the court, inspire the
court. They speak for you though now you speak for them.

PAULET. You don't know the verdict already do you?

MARY. In as much as Lord Burleigh is here to deliver it, yes I do. So let's get on with it.

BURLEIGH. You submitted yourself to trial by forty judges, my lady.

MARY. I'll stop you there. Firstly, I submitted myself to nothing. It's set down in English law, is it not, that the accused shall be judged by his peers? But who in that committee was my peer? Only crowned kings are my equals, no-one else.

BURLEIGH. Excuse me, but you heard the charges, you allowed the process of law.

MARY. Yes I lent half an ear to your charges, but only out of honour, in the certainty that their fraudulence would be exposed. I respect their Lordships' persons, to a point, but not their office.

BURLEIGH. Whether you do or not is an empty formality, which need hardly hinder the process of the law. You are on English soil, breathing English air, you enjoy the protection of its laws, thus you are also under English jurisdiction.

MARY. I'm beneath the English soil, breathing the air of an English dungeon. I am not a subject of England, I am the monarch of a neighbouring power. And as for English laws, I hardly know them, still less seek their protection.

BURLEIGH. So you think that title gives you licence to foment civil war in other countries – and to go unpunished?

MARY. I still respect the rule of law – it's merely your judges I reject.

BURLEIGH. My judges? I beg your pardon, my lady. Do you think they are mere lackeys, hired tongues? They are the first and finest of the land. Strong enough to be above ambition, faction or corruption.

MARY. Your eloquence is stirring. How could I, a mere woman and unlettered, compete with such an orator?
    Believe me, if these Lords were as you describe them, I would bow myself to their decision, and my cause would be in vain – provided of course that they were to find me guilty. But this cabal of famous names who hope by their combined weight to pulverise me, I don't quite see them as you do. They seem to me to play a different part. I see the English aristocracy, the

House of Lords and other assorted knights as no more than
eunuchs in the sultan's palace. And that sultan was my great
uncle, Henry the Eighth. And since his time the House of Lords
has scurried about like servants below stairs, busily making and
repealing laws, dissolving marriages and reforming them, at
their master's whim – disinheriting an English Princess one
day, calling her a bastard even, then crowning her as Queen the
next. These noble and incorruptible peers – I've seen them,
with equal if transmutable conviction, change their religion four
times under four different regimes.

BURLEIGH. For one who cannot understand our laws you seem
particularly well versed in our misfortunes!

MARY. . . . and these are to be my judges! Lord Burleigh, I will be
fair with you – will you be just to me? They say you work
tirelessly and incorruptibly for the good of the State. It may be
so. I hope it is. They say that you're not swayed by private
greed, but rather by your sovereign and your country's good.
Not everyone is so honest. No doubt there are some honourable
men among my judges. But they are Protestants, fanatics,
British Nationalists, and they denounce me, Queen of Scotland,
as a papist. And the British can never be just to the Scottish.
How can they, the history of bloodshed is too long and too
bitter. And will never end until one Parliament, one sceptre
holds total sway, and brings us both together.

BURLEIGH. And a Stuart can achieve all this?

MARY. I hope so. I can't deny it's always been my dream. To
dowse the flames of these ancient wars. And to forge our
crowns into an orb of peace.

BURLEIGH. And look how you go about it. You aim to set this
land on fire and, striding through the flames, ascend the throne.

MARY. That isn't true – I swear it by Almighty God. When did I
plot against England, where is the proof?

BURLEIGH. It was decided – forty votes to two – that you broke
our law.

MARY. A law made in haste expressly to condemn me.

BURLEIGH. Not to condemn you but to warn you. That if tumult
was raised in your name, your life would be forfeit. You knew
this, you saw the danger – and still you plotted with Babington
and his henchmen. You knew their every move – you led the
plot from prison.

MARY. When? Show me the evidence.

BURLEIGH. You saw the documents at your trial.

MARY. Copies in a hand unknown to me. Bring me proof that
I dictated them as they appeared in court.

BURLEIGH. Babington confessed that they were genuine. Shortly
before his untimely death.

MARY. Why didn't you call him as a living witness? Why was he
shuffled from the world with such despatch? What were you
afraid of?

BURLEIGH. Your secretaries, your loyal servants swore the
documents were just as you dictated them.

MARY. Every servant is loyal until put to the test. And torture is
the cruellest test of all.

BURLEIGH. They swore it with their own free will.

MARY. But not in front of me. Two witnesses, both still alive – so
bring them here – let them repeat their testimony to my face.
This is my right by English law – you wouldn't deny it to a
murderer, then why to me? Am I wrong? This is my right, is it
not? Paulet, you are honest, you tell me.

PAULET. It is, my lady. I can't deny the truth.

MARY. Well then. Since you insist on the letter of the law, so
will I. Tell me, why wasn't Babington called to court before
my eyes? And my two clerks, I presume they're still alive,
where are they now?

BURLEIGH. You're merely exciting yourself. Your plot with
Babington is not the only matter . . .

MARY. It's the only charge with which I've been accused by law.
I will not let you wriggle out of this. You stick to the point.

BURLEIGH. It's proved that you had dealings with Mendoza, the
Spanish Ambassador . . .

MARY. Stick to the point.

BURLEIGH. And that you plotted the overthrow of the true
religion of this land, conspiring with all the Kings of Europe.

MARY. And suppose I did? I'm not saying that I did, but suppose
I did, what then?

> You hold me here illegally in prison
> In flagrant breach of every country's law.
> I didn't come to England sword in hand
> I came here as a suppliant and to beg
> For sanctuary and help; and so I threw
> Myself upon the mercy of your Queen,
> My blood relation and my only hope,
> But I was seized and put in chains and left.
> So tell me in all conscience should I graft
> All my love and loyalty to England?
> What has England ever done for me . . .
> So when I try to burst free from these chains
> I exercise a higher rule of law
> Which all of the rest of Europe knows and honours,
> So let them fight for me and my just cause
> And if a war ensues that war is just.
> But England isn't interested in justice.

BURLEIGH. I'm afraid you can't invoke these higher principles
  my lady. Not as our prisoner.

MARY. No, I am weak and she is strong – so be it.
  Let her use force and wipe me out, but then
  Admit the deed was done with force not justice.
  She mustn't hide her sword from the high court
  Or wear the gaudy robes of virtue while
  Disposing of her enemies by stealth.
  Pure hypocrisy . . .
  Which wouldn't fool the world for one small minute.
  Don't sweep your dirty-work behind the courts,
  Elizabeth, or the church. Rather dare
  To show yourself exactly as you are.

  Exit.

Act One Scene Eight

BURLEIGH. She's mocking us, Paulet, and will continue to mock
  us till her head's on the block. A proud heart cannot easily be
  broken. Did you see how calmly she heard the sentence? Did
  she weep, or even change colour? And clever, too. Not to
  invoke our sympathy but rather the Queen's lack of resolve.

Our fear gives her strength.

PAULET. Even so, there have been irregularities. We should have let her face Babington in court – we should call her secretaries. We still can . . .

BURLEIGH. No. Never. You've seen how manipulative she can be. Her sorcery may well confuse the witnesses – they may forget their testimony . . .

PAULET. But as it is our enemies will start to spread malicious rumours. And all the trappings of our court will seem a trumped-up travesty.

BURLEIGH. I know it. And so does the Queen. God, if only this serpent had been trampled under foot before she slithered into England.

PAULET. Amen to that.

BURLEIGH. Or if she'd sickened and died in prison.

PAULET. If only . . .

BURLEIGH. But again, if she'd died of natural causes, we'd only be thought the murderers.

PAULET. People will think what they want to think.

BURLEIGH. How could we prove we hadn't killed her? Or indeed, they prove we had? But still, at the same time it is unthinkable that she should live. And that's the point, and that's why Elizabeth is robbed of her sleep. I can read her torment in her eyes. She cannot dare express her wish in words; but her eyes are unambiguous. Her servants are negligent, every one of them.

PAULET. Negligent?

BURLEIGH. They take no notice of her unspoken orders.

PAULET. What do you mean?

BURLEIGH. The commands she cannot give. You're right, there is a serpent in our Kingdom – so why protect it like a precious jewel?

PAULET. The only precious jewel I know is my sovereign's name – which can't be too closely guarded. But next to that there's my own reputation – and my honour – it was surely for them that I was made Mary's jailer.

BURLEIGH. Mary may fall ill, who knows? We'll say she has, she'll fade away in men's minds and then in truth and then your reputation will remain intact.

PAULET. But not my conscience.

BURLEIGH. Don't worry, you wouldn't need to lend your hand. But you might be required to turn your back.

PAULET. No murderer will ever enter here. Her life is in my hands – and it is no less holy than that of my own Queen. You are her judges – then judge her. When the time is right, I'll open my gates to the carpenters and scaffolders, to sheriffs, even to executioners. To justice and the rigmarole of justice. But not to murder. I've sworn to keep her, to guard her, and to be sure she does no harm – nor comes to any either. Farewell.

Exit.

Act Two Scene One

The Palace of Westminster.

DAVISON. My Lord of Kent, are you back already, and are the festivities over?

KENT. Weren't you there? Why not?

DAVISON. I was at my work . . .

KENT. Well you missed the most delightful, the most sumptuous spectacle. An allegory. The Fortress of Beauty – besieged by 'desire'. First a herald appeared to serenade the fortress with a madrigal and the chancellor sang back from the ramparts (enough to frighten *anyone* away). Then the artillery fired volleys of flowers and perfumed pomanders rained down like cannon balls. But all in vain. The scented onslaught was repulsed and desire withdrew, his tail between his legs.

DAVISON. This hardly bodes well for the Queen's betrothal.

KENT. Don't be silly, it's just a bit of fun. And I think the fortress will crumble in time.

DAVISON. Do you think so? I'm not so sure.

KENT. The country fears one thing – that she should die without an heir and the Stuart woman should ascend the throne with her darling, the Pope, in tow.

DAVISON. Never. Elizabeth is bound for her marriage bed. Mary merely for her tomb.

KENT. The Queen!

Act Two Scene Two

ELIZABETH *joins, led by* LEICESTER, *the French Ambassador,*
LORD BURLEIGH. *Other French and English Lords. Also*
BELLIEVRE.

ELIZABETH. My dear Aubespine! Sir, your noble friends
    Who've come so far must not feel disappointed.
    Our paltry entertainments must seem dull
    When set against the court of St. Germain,
    You French are so gallant and so unbuttoned,
    You crowd around my carriage, blessing me
    Quite openly. Delightful. This poor spectacle
    Was all I had to offer. Not the array
    Of France's fairest maidens, which I hear
    Grow in Queen Katherine's pleasure gardens.
    Imagine me among a thousand beauties,
    I love plays, but I hate to be upstaged.

AUBESPINE. There's but one flower which blooms in
                              Westminster
    And you are she, and you are all your sex
    A thousand women's beauty in quintessence.

ELIZABETH. Oh, ambassador, really.

BELLIEVRE. So says Monsieur, our royal Lord. And he
    Regrets his absence. Still he is not far
    Away – he merely waits your royal word,
    The word is 'yes'.

ELIZABETH. Bellievre, that will do.
    I've said the time is not yet ripe, to light
    The torch of holy matrimony. These are
    Dark times – dark and dangerous . . .

BELLIEVRE. A promise
    Would be enough your majesty. Then happier
    Days will follow when that promise is fulfilled.

ELIZABETH. Alas. Kings and queens are nothing more
    Than slaves. We cannot follow our own hearts.
    I'd always wished to die unmarried, hoped
    That that would be my fame, that on my grave
    The world would read 'Here lies the virgin queen'
    But my subjects just won't have it, they insist
    That one day I'll be gone, 'What then?' they say.
    Ungrateful bunch, they should rejoice that we

Are happy and at peace and not compel me
To sacrifice my virtue to the future,
To yield my dearest gift up to the state.
And have a lord and master thrust upon me
As it were – though this is England's will
It feels like a reproach, a cruel reminder
That I'm a woman; nothing but a woman.
And I'd intended I should rule this nation
Like a king – and like a man. Ah well!
I know it's an offence to God to stand
The laws of nature on their head. But should
A woman who spends every day in toil,
In ceaseless, willing labour for her country
Not be exempt from that function which
However natural it is, still makes
Half of the world subservient to the other?

AUBESPINE. On your throne you epitomise and glorify
Every single virtue, every one,
You are the pearl of your whole sex, the very
Paradigm of all that Woman is.
No man on earth is worthy to receive
That sacrifice of your freedom. None
But if there were such a man, if his birth
Allowed it, if virtue, honour . . .

ELIZABETH. No, really,
There's no better resting-place
For that most precious jewel, my freedom,
Than in France . . . Or rather
That sacrifice would injure me the least,
And that's as much as I'm prepared to say.

BELLIEVRE. How generous, how full of hope. Monsieur
However, hopes for something more than hope.

ELIZABETH. What, for example? This? (*Her ring.*) Funny, the
same symbol for all of womankind, the queen or the fishwife –
the same sign of duty and subservience. Rings to forge a
marriage, rings to forge a chain.

BELLIEVRE. In his name, mighty Queen, I kneel and accept this
gift. Let me pay homage to my princess with a kiss . . .

ELIZABETH (*admonishing, to* LEICESTER *who is staring at
her*). My Lord Leicester . . . (*Then to the others.*) Let all
suspicion between our two nations disappear, and may a bond
be forged between our crowns, between France and Britain.

AUBESPINE. What a day of joy this is for both our nations. A day of peace and of sunshine. If only one small ray could fall upon that most unhappy princess . . .

ELIZABETH. And that's a different matter altogether. If France wishes to be allied to us, she should also share all my concerns and not befriend my enemies.

AUBESPINE. You will agree, I trust, that we would be acting dishonourably if we neglected a friend in need, one of our religion, the widow of our former King. No, sheer humanity forbids it.

ELIZABETH. You must do as your humanity dictates. Allow me, however, to act as a queen.

They bow and exeunt.

Act Two Scene Three

ELIZABETH, LEICESTER, BURLEIGH *and* TALBOT *are left.*

BURLEIGH. Glorious queen to your nation, the happy day has arrived where your people can sigh with relief and enjoy their present blessings without fretting for the future. No more storm clouds. Or rather, only one. Only one sacrifice that all England demands. Agree to that and this day will be remembered for all eternity.

ELIZABETH. Well, what do they desire, tell me?

BURLEIGH. The Stuart woman's head. And nothing less.

As you know, not all Britons think alike. The Church of Rome numbers many secret zealots on this island. And they have murderous thoughts in their hearts, and they worship her. They send spies to these shores, sworn fanatics variously disguised – murderer on murderer. We intercept them, of course, but the gaping maw of Rome and of Rheims provides an endless flow of enemies to us.

And the genius of this eternal war, the spider of this web of intrigue squats in Fotheringay Castle. They follow her, to certain death, of course, and still she eggs them on. The motto of this doomed generation is 'Free Mary, put her on the throne'.

Your throne. For them, you've stolen the throne, or it's yours
by chance or trickery or something. They plot for her, it was
they who made her dub herself Queen of England. There is no
peace with them, or her, or any of her kindred.

ELIZABETH. My Lord, you hold a high and heavy office. I know
how zealously you strive for me, and indeed that there is
wisdom in your words. But wisdom which calls for blood, is
wisdom I detest. Can't you temper your advice? Lord Talbot,
what do you think?

TALBOT. May you live long, your Majesty, the pride of your
people; this is a happy golden age, we haven't seen its like for
many years. Let us hope we don't forfeit our happiness if and
when we forfeit our good name. Or at least let Talbot's eyes be
shut, when this bloody deed is being done.

ELIZABETH. God forbid we should blacken our name.

TALBOT. In which case we must find another way, a lawful way,
to save the kingdom. For this execution would be unjust and be
seen to be unjust. She is not your subject, and thus not subject
to your laws.

ELIZABETH. So all my parliament, and my ministers were
wrong? Every court in the land – who found unanimously that
right was on my side?

TALBOT. Unanimity is no proof of right or wrong. England is not
the world, your parliament is not a league of nations. Don't say
you're mirroring the passions of your people; don't talk of
necessity. Or rather do, but exercise your own free will. If you
hate bloodshed, then say so. Publicly say you want to save your
cousin's life – and if you wish to show your royal wrath then
turn it on those who advise you otherwise. You must rule, and
you alone must rule. Follow your own feelings – and if they're
soft and forgiving, so be it – God didn't create woman to be
strong. Their hearts are weak and easily led – as Mary was in
her dark time, when she threw herself into Bothwell's arms –
for her weakness desired his strength . . .

ELIZABETH. Not every woman is weak. Watch your words; I'll
hear no more of this weakness of our sex.

TALBOT. Lust blinded her, disabled her – and she was born away
on a stream of corruption; of course her beauty worked to her
advantage, she outstripped every other woman – in grace and in
birth . . .

ELIZABETH. Talbot, please, control yourself – this is the privy
council, not a house of pleasure . . . But she must be fair indeed
if she can heat an old man's blood to boiling point . . .
Leicester, nothing to add? Does his eloquence inhibit yours?

LEICESTER. I'm just amazed, your Majesty, struck dumb. That
scaremongers can be allowed to cram your ears with tittle-tattle,
fairy tales; good for frightening the rabble in the London
streets, but hardly – excuse me – fit for the Council Chamber.
I'm just astonished that this Queen of Nowhere, who couldn't
even command her own tiny kingdom; pushed out by her own
people, imprisoned – and quite rightly – for years, should
occasion you a moment's anxiety. What, in Heaven's name,
have you to fear? That England, in its hour of peace should rush
into the arms of this papist, that they'd desert you, born and
bred and honoured as a queen in favour of a murderess? What
are these fainthearts doing, who wish to frogmarch you – I use
the word advisedly – to the altar and yes, safeguard the state
and church; but from what? Not, I'm sure, from her, withering
away in prison while you are in the glory of your youth. You
will, I trust, pay many visits to her grave, lay the odd wreath,
who knows, without having to first push her into it.

BURLEIGH. Of course, this wasn't always your opinion.

LEICESTER. Indeed, I asked for her death in the court – but not in
the Council Chamber. Here we talk of expediency, not justice.
Why kill the woman? She's already dead.
Indifference is death – and so's contempt.
Martyrdom would merely resurrect her.
Here's my advice – you let the sentence stand
In fullest force – that she's condemned to death.
Then let her live, and live beneath the axe,
The headsman's blade two inches from her neck -
One hint of insurrection – let it fall.

ELIZABETH. My Lords, I thank you for your learned counsel,
Your zeal, your devotion and your candour.
Almighty God will hence forth be my guide,
I'll pray to Him – then do what I think best.

Act Two Scene Four

Enter PAULET *and* MORTIMER.

ELIZABETH. Amias Paulet. And who is this?

PAULET. Your radiant Majesty. My nephew, recently returned
from long voyages abroad, has come to abase himself at your
feet. May you receive him with indulgence and mercy, and may
he prosper in the sunshine of your favour.

MORTIMER. Long life to my noble Queen and may peace and joy
bedeck her brow forever.

ELIZABETH. Arise sir. You are welcome to England. I hear you
were in France, in Rome and Rheims. Tell me, what plots are
our enemies hatching?

MORTIMER. At present there's much confusion in their ranks.
Now France has signed treaties of solidarity with us – they can
turn only to Spain.

ELIZABETH. Yes, I know. Walsingham told me as much.

MORTIMER. And a Bull from Pope Sixtus, against yourself, has
come from Rome, and just arrived in Rheims as I was setting
sail.

LEICESTER. These letters hardly frighten England any more. I
rather think the bull has lost its horns!

BURLEIGH. In a fanatic's hands it is a deadly weapon, never
doubt it.

ELIZABETH (*observing* MORTIMER *closely*). Have you been
blamed for visiting the colleges in Rheims and forswearing
your true faith?

MORTIMER. Well, it's true – I did forswear my faith – or
seemingly I did – such was my desire to serve your Majesty.

ELIZABETH (*to* PAULET). And what is this, Paulet?

PAULET. A letter – sent to you – by the Queen of Scots.

BURLEIGH (*snatching it*). I'll take care of that.

PAULET. Forgive me, Lord Treasurer, but the lady told me to
deliver this into the Queen's hands only. She thinks I'm her
sworn enemy. I'm enemy only to her crimes – if she
commands, I will obey her, if that's consistent with my duty.

Meanwhile the Queen is reading the letter.

BURLEIGH. What is in it? Do you know?

PAULET. She told me what was in it. She asks permission for an audience with the Queen.

BURLEIGH. Never!

PAULET. Why not? The request is just.

BURLEIGH. She has forfeited the right to see the Queen by plotting her overthrow and her death – we cannot let her near her.

TALBOT. If the Queen were moved to mercy, would you still stand in her way?

BURLEIGH. Mary's condemned to death. If the Queen should see her, then the sentence cannot be enforced, for the royal presence implies a royal pardon – and that cannot be . . .

ELIZABETH (*visibly moved*). What is life? And what is
happiness
On earth? See how a mighty Queen can fall.
Her life began with so much pride and hope
Which called her to the oldest throne in Christendom
So old and great that in her mind she wore
Three crowns. She spoke a different language then,
Oh yes, quite different when she dared
To put the arms of England on her flag
And spurred by flatterers allowed herself
To be dubbed queen of all the British Isles.
Excuse me, my Lords, my soul is torn in two.
My heart weeps blood, my eyes bleed tears. For
Nothing is solid on this earth – nothing.
Man's fate is dreadful, black and dreadful,
And its shadow, even now, sweeps over me
And passes on . . . Thank God.

TALBOT. Your Majesty! God has moved your heart to pity.
Listen to its voice. Reach out your hand and help her to her
feet; shine your holy light into her darkest dungeon.

BURLEIGH. Do nothing of the kind, your Majesty. By which
I mean do not let your good nature, which God knows is to be
praised, lead you astray. You can't pardon her, or save her –
we have come too far for that. And if you saw her all the world
would blame you and say you merely wished to gloat over your
victim and laugh at her despair.

LEICESTER. Perhaps we've all said enough. The Queen is wise

to listen to her own heart, and not to our poor council.
Nevertheless, two queens may meet, and debate and still not
affect the law. And it was England, not Elizabeth, who
condemned her. Perhaps – who knows – it's to her Majesty's
credit that she follows the gentler feelings of her heart – while
justice still pursues its rigorous ends.

ELIZABETH. Enough, my Lords, enough. We'll try to steer
A fitting middle course – if such there be –
Between mercy and dire necessity.
Now leave me.

They leave.

Mortimer. One word with you.

Act Two Scene Five

ELIZABETH. Young man, you have a self-possession far beyond
your years. One already so adept in the art of deception is most
advanced in his apprenticeship and ripe before his time. Fate
has great things in store for you – this is my prophecy. And my
prophecies, you'll find, have a habit of coming true.

MORTIMER. Great Queen – everything I am and am to be is
dedicated only to your service.

ELIZABETH. You know our enemies well. You've lived among
them. You'll have seen that their hatred for me is quite
implacable and their capacity for mischief inexhaustible. Now
the Almighty, in his mercy, has kept me safe so far. But my
royal crown will never sit securely on my head as long as she's
alive to encourage these wild fanatics, to inflame both them and
their desire.

MORTIMER. You've but to say the word and she's no more . . .

ELIZABETH. Ah! I thought I'd made myself clear. Never mind.
Let's try again, in plainer speech this time. I'd hoped the courts
of justice would have washed my hands quite clean of any
lingering, polluting stain of blood. And in a sense they have –
they've spoken their sentence. But only I can authorise the
execution. Then the weight of horror and opprobrium will fall
directly on my shoulders. You see the problem. I have to seem

to be responsible and yet maintain the appearance of
detachment.

MORTIMER. But if the deed is just, why worry about
appearances?

ELIZABETH. I don't think you understand the world. Not yet,
anyway. We are always judged on what we seem to be – never
on what we are. Merely to be right is neither here nor there; and
won't convince a soul. No, it's essential that my part in her
death should seem in doubt. Ambiguous. And the only true
protection for such deeds is darkness and obscurity. Seen but
unseen.

MORTIMER. Then perhaps it would be best . . .

ELIZABETH. Perhaps it would. Oh yes, my guardian angel's
speaking through your voice. Carry on, speak your mind. I know
you understand. You're quite a different man from your uncle.

MORTIMER. My uncle? Did you tell him of your wishes?

ELIZABETH. I did. And now I regret it.

MORTIMER. Forgive him your Majesty. Bold deeds like this
require a young man's hand.

ELIZABETH. Then will you . . . ?

MORTIMER. My hand is yours – if you can protect your noble
name.

ELIZABETH. Good – yes, very good. So, if one morning, quite
soon, you were to wake me up with the sweet news that my
cousin, my bloody enemy had passed away in the night, well,
then I'd . . .

MORTIMER. Majesty – you can count on me.

ELIZABETH. Splendid. So when will my head lie easily on my
pillow?

MORTIMER. By the next full moon. By then you'll sleep much
more soundly.

ELIZABETH. Then fare you well – my gratitude will be
considerable – but, alas and perforce – completely secret, or
rather, better expressed under cover of darkness. But then
again, the closest, sweetest bonds are often forged in secret,
isn't that so?

Exit.

Act Two Scene Six

MORTIMER. Yes – off you go. You vile, lubricious, double-dealing queen. As you deceive the world, so I do you. And it'll be an honour to betray you. Why choose me? Do I look like a murderer? Do you see a lust for killing in my eyes? No, you want to borrow my strong young hands to do your dirty work. My Lady Bountiful – beaming with grace and clemency – but rotten with hypocrisy inside – secretly enjoying every private thrust of the dagger. Well, perhaps I've sold my soul – but think of what I've bought. Time – time to be sure of her rescue. But meanwhile, Elizabeth, you drop such succulent hints of my eventual reward – my elevation to your side, your favour, your very person – but in vain, foolish woman, what have you to offer me? Ha! What a temptress – a grinning Eve with a maggot-ridden apple.

Suddenly uneasy.

I have to stay here and deliver this to my Lord of Leicester. Him? Damn – damn, I hate waiting. I wasn't meant to be a courtier, but . . .

Only I can rescue her – who else would even dare?
The danger! The fame – and, oh, the prize beyond compare.

Act Two Scene Seven

MORTIMER. Uncle.

PAULET. What has she said to you?

MORTIMER. Oh, nothing, nothing of importance.

PAULET. You listen to me. This is a dangerous game, believe me. Greed and ambition can easily overreach themselves and topple headlong.

MORTIMER. You brought me to the court – why else if not for my preferment – if that is ambition, then you and I have it in common.

PAULET. I wish to God I'd never brought you here. Some things can be hidden, but your conscience will always find you out.

MORTIMER. I don't know what you're talking about.

PAULET. Beware. Whatever she may promise you, whatever giddy heights or whatever else, beware her flattering tongue. For believe me, if you obey her dark desires she'll disown you, no, worse than that, she'll seek revenge and punish you for the very deed, the murder that she's ordered you to perform.

MORTIMER. What murder do you mean, what deed? I don't understand.

PAULET. Come on, let's not play games. I know what she desires from you. So, nephew, what did you say? What did you tell her?

MORTIMER. Uncle.

PAULET. Because if you concurred, if you said 'yes', then I'll cast you down, reject you as my own, and curse you forever, until . . .

LEICESTER (*enters suddenly*). I'm terribly sorry – is this a bad time? Because if it is, I can always . . . I just wanted a quick word with your nephew. Our Sovereign Queen is particularly impressed with him. Most gratifying – apparently she wishes him to have full and sole custody of the Lady Stuart. She admires his probity, it seems, and trusts him absolutely.

PAULET. Trusts him? Ha!

LEICESTER. I beg your pardon?

PAULET. The Queen may trust him, but I trust only myself, my instincts and these unsleeping eyes.

Exit.

Act Two Scene Eight

LEICESTER. Oh dear, what's got into him?

MORTIMER. Perhaps surprise and joy at my sudden advancement. The queen's put so much trust in me, and not in him.

LEICESTER. That may be. But tell me, are you deserving of such trust? (*Looking intently at him.*) Or, to put it plainly, are you a man who can be trusted?

MORTIMER (*returning his gaze*). Perhaps I should ask the same of you, Lord Leicester?

LEICESTER. You have something to say to me in private.

MORTIMER. Perhaps I do – but first I must be sure that it is prudent.

LEICESTER. And meanwhile, how can I be sure of you? You mustn't be offended. I'm not mistrustful by nature, but I notice things. I notice you, for instance, showing two faces at court. One of them by definition is false – but I wonder which.

MORTIMER. Precisely the question which I would ask of you, Lord Leicester.

LEICESTER. Well. Here we both are. Which of us should make the first move?

MORTIMER. Perhaps the man who runs less risk.

LEICESTER. Perhaps. Which would be you, I think.

MORTIMER. No, surely you. A word from you to the powers-that-be would strike me dead. In an instant. No accusation from me could ever come near you, nor touch you, your fame or your favour.

LEICESTER. That's where you're wrong. I'm the weakest man at court – the merest whisper of a rumour would unseat me.

MORTIMER. Your influence, your power are legendary. If you dare to reveal to me a chink in your proud armour – then, God help me, I must take my cue and follow your example. And speak honestly.

LEICESTER. You go first – and if I can, I'll follow you.

MORTIMER (*produces the letter*). Very well. This is for you – from the Queen of Scotland.

LEICESTER. Damn you, keep your voice down. Ah! Her picture, a letter from her fair hand.

MORTIMER. Now I believe you.

LEICESTER. Do you know what's in this letter?

MORTIMER. I know nothing.

LEICESTER. She must have told you.

MORTIMER. She's told me nothing. How can the Earl of Leicester, Elizabeth's darling, Mary's sworn enemy, one of the

very men who judged her, who condemned her, be the thing
that she describes as her salvation? But it's plainly so – your
eyes show quite clearly your feelings for her.

LEICESTER. First tell me about yourself – why have you thrust
your hand into the flame?

MORTIMER. I've forsworn my faith and turned to Rome. A letter
from the Archbishop of Rheims ensured my credit with the
Queen of Scotland.

LEICESTER. I've heard about your change of faith. Which is why
I dared to trust you. I'm sorry – give me your hand – I'm sorry
to have doubted you. But caution is everything. Burleigh and
Walsingham hate me, and set traps for me at every turning. You
could have been a spy, a double agent, sent to find me out – it
wouldn't be unheard of.

MORTIMER. I always thought you bestrode this court like a
warrior, in fact you can only proceed in tiny steps, I pity you
for that.

LEICESTER. You might think this a sudden change of heart – it's
not – I'd never hated Mary – the times required it. You know
she was once intended for me – oh this is years ago, before
Darnley, before her fall from glory. But I was so ambitious that
I could not see the jewel I'd been offered. Mary's hand was too
small a gift for me, it was Elizabeth or nothing.

MORTIMER. She famously prefers you to all other men.

LEICESTER. Yes, so they say, but ten long years of hollow
courtship was sheer slavery. Ten years spent in flattering her
vanity, applauding every change of her heart, at the whim of her
whimsy, one minute fondled like a cocker spaniel, then kicked
off like a mongrel with the mange. Plagued equally by her
anger and her affection, hemmed about by her jealousy, scolded
like a five-year-old, abused like a half-witted valet. Hell, pure
hell. And all – now – for nothing!

MORTIMER. Surely not.

LEICESTER. My rightful prize snatched away from me, at the
very moment of victory – after so many years of service – this
cocky juvenile turns up and forces me, the leading man, to
leave the stage – the scene of all my triumphs. Her hand, her
favour are both slipping away from me – all to him, the upstart
Monsieur; but what hope have I – he's presentable, more than
presentable and she's a female . . .

MORTIMER. And he's Katherine's son – so he's learned flattery and statecraft from the best.

LEICESTER. A complete disaster, the shipwreck of my hopes. So, I look for a piece of wreckage I can cling to, a fragment of joy – and I remember Mary. And then, all her everything floods back to me in shining torrent; ambition had blinded my heart – now I compare the two, I see that I have tossed aside a priceless jewel, and set my heart on dross. You see, all her misery had stemmed from me, my fault – thus it was for me to mend. That's how my plan, my dream began – to rescue her and make her mine.

MORTIMER. Rescue her? Excuse me, what have you done to rescue her? You've let her be sentenced to death, you even voted against her. But everything's in hand. She'll soon be free. And now your support makes us certain of success.

LEICESTER. What? You can't . . .

MORTIMER. We can, we'll break open her prison, my followers are ready and waiting.

LEICESTER. Your followers, others, men who know the plan? What are you doing? Are you mad? Do they know about me?

MORTIMER. Our plan was forged before I knew your secret – we can rescue her without your help.

LEICESTER. So you're sure my name has never even been mentioned in connection with this plot?

MORTIMER. Look I've come to help you, to fight your cause. You wish to save Mary, and to claim her; now help's arrived, you've many friends you didn't know you had; you might look a little happier about it.

LEICESTER. Force can achieve nothing. It's too dangerous to attempt.

MORTIMER. More dangerous not to . . .

LEICESTER. If we fail, we drag her down with us.

MORTIMER. And if we don't take risks, she won't be saved.

LEICESTER. You're not thinking, not listening – merely lashing out, undoing everything, all my good . . .

MORTIMER. All your good work! And what good work is that? What single step have you taken to save her? And how would you, for example – if I were vile enough to obey Elizabeth's orders and have her murdered – how would you or your non-existent followers save her then?

LEICESTER. She ordered you to murder?

MORTIMER. She mistook her man, as Mary did with you.

LEICESTER. And what did you say? Did you agree?

MORTIMER. I did – to stop her asking someone else.

LEICESTER. Good – the sentence won't be carried out, not yet and we'll have gained some time . . .

MORTIMER. Enough of this, we're losing time . . .

LEICESTER. No, no. And let me think: the more she's counting on you to do her dirty work, the more she'll want to appear great and merciful. So perhaps I can convince her, somehow, that she should meet her enemy face to face, and be seen to be gracious – and then of course, Burleigh is right, the sentence can't ever be carried out. Yes it's possible, but how best to lay the ground . . .

MORTIMER. But what'll that achieve? Nothing will have changed. You'd have to use force eventually, so why not use it at the outset? You are Elizabeth's favourite, lure her to your castle, you've done it before – then show your true mettle. Imprison her, and hold her hostage until Queen Mary is released.

LEICESTER. You're completely mad. And I'm mad to be even talking to you. Don't you know the thrall in which she holds the court and thus the kingdom? The reign of terror. All our spirits manacled and shackled. The heroes are all dead, everything's turned to dust, the few brave men are corrupted and under her thumb, no one dares speak a word. Follow my advice, say nothing, do nothing until I . . . someone's coming . . . Quick.

MORTIMER. Mary's waiting for your reply. What shall I say?

LEICESTER. Tell her I swear to love her forever.

MORTIMER. Tell her yourself. I'll not be your go-between.

Exit.

Act Two Scene Nine

ELIZABETH. Who was that? I heard voices.

LEICESTER. Sir Mortimer.

ELIZABETH. Lord Leicester, something's wrong?

LEICESTER. No, nothing's wrong.
    It's just . . .
    I've never seen you looking quite so radiant,
    Your beauty's blinding me and oh . . .

ELIZABETH. What is it?

LEICESTER. When I see your fair face, all your charms
    I think of everything I've lost . . .

ELIZABETH. You've lost?

LEICESTER. Yes lost. Your heart, your love, yourself, for soon
    You'll languish in your hot young husband's arms
    And he will have your undivided heart
    And I'll have nothing. He's never seen you. He
    Can only love your crown, your reputation
    I love you for yourself. If I were King
    Of all the world and you a shepherdess
    I'd worship at your cottage every day
    And lay out all my riches at your feet.
    It's hard that you won't do as much for me.

ELIZABETH. It is. Well nigh unbearable. So Dudley
    Pity me, don't scold me. I'm not allowed
    To listen to my heart. And if I were
    You know that I'd have chosen otherwise.
    My God, I envy other women who
    Can glorify the object of their love
    Make him master, worship him. But I
    Can never raise you to my level. I
    Can never give my crown to you, the man
    I love most in the world. But she was free with
    Her fortune and her favours. Yes, Mary did
    Exactly as she pleased, with whomsoever
    She pleased. She even gave her royal crown
    As if it were the merest lover's bauble.
    She drank the cup of pleasure to the dregs

LEICESTER. She drinks the cup of sorrow now. Remorse.

ELIZABETH. She didn't care a jot what people said
    Or thought. Which makes it easy. Easy to
    Live and love – and how I envy her.
    Her freedom now – I mean her freedom then.
    I had to strive to be a King while she
    Strove but to be a woman. Half the world,
    The young and old were all in love with her.
    Just like men – so shallow, so debauched,
    That any girlish nonsense turns their brains
    And earns their silly admiration.
    Pathetic. You saw how Talbot simpered
    Like a love-sick boy when we discussed her.

LEICESTER. He had to guard her once; you should forgive him.
    She probably ensnared him with her charms.

ELIZABETH. But is she really so very beautiful?
    I've heard the stories, I've been forced to hear them,
    But now and then I've wondered what the truth is.
    Painters flatter, portraits lie . . . I wonder -
    I'd only trust my own eyes. What's the matter?

LEICESTER. Nothing. No nothing. Your Highness
    I'd love to see her face when she sees yours –
    Then she would see, for jealous eyes see best,
    The nobility of you. And she would know
    That she had lost the battle, yes, that battle
    Along with all the others . . .

ELIZABETH. Still she's younger.

LEICESTER. Younger! What's that? And who'd ever guess it?
    She's suffered, life has made her bitter and
    Ill-favoured. And what could be more bitter
    Or rather sweet, than seeing you a bride.
    And more than just a bride, a bride of France,
    Which makes the irony the more delicious,
    Doubly so, because she dares to pin
    Her future hopes on France.

ELIZABETH. I don't know.
    There's pressure from all sides that I should see her.

LEICESTER. Then see her. Why not? She begs it as
    A favour. Do it as a punishment –
    The final blow, the final execution –
    To see the famous torch of Mary's beauty
    Dowsed by yours . . . by your presence.

Just now, when you came in, I told you, I
Was almost blinded. Well imagine walking
Unannounced into her prison cell.
Your radiance would shrivel up her eyes.

ELIZABETH. Yes. No. Not now. I can't – I must be careful.
Lord Burleigh says . . .

LEICESTER. Lord Burleigh cares only for
Affairs of state. But the fact that you're a woman
Means you have special rights. Rights of your own.
Enforce them. You are more than just a Queen.
Why should your majesty obscure your sex?
. . . not only that – perhaps it would be statesmanlike
– Lord Burleigh might approve – if you performed
A public act of generosity
And under that disguise enjoy your triumph.

ELIZABETH. If I saw her in prison and in penury
Perhaps it might appear that I was gloating
If I appeared in majesty, while she
Is stripped of everything . . .

LEICESTER. Of course you're right
But there's a way. You do not even need
To cross her threshold. Fortune's on our side.
Tomorrow is the Hunt – and Fotheringay
May well be on our route – and then who knows –
The Stuart woman may be walking in the park,
And you may come across her quite by chance,
Or seemingly by chance. But if it suits you
You needn't speak to her at all.

ELIZABETH. If this is a mistake, Lord Leicester, it will be
Your mistake, not mine, remember that.
Your desire, which I fulfil to please you.
Because I've done you wrong, I know I have . . .
So all the world will see this as it is –
A silly whim of yours, and yours alone.
A thing which I'll indulge, but not condone.

Act Three Scene One

The Park of Fotheringay Castle.

KENNEDY. Wait – stop – I can't keep up. You've not behaved like this since you were tiny.

MARY. I know, I know. But let me enjoy it – let me be a child again . . . let me skip across the meadows, let me fly, let me gulp the fresh, clean air. And forget we were ever anything but – free!!

KENNEDY. Dear lady – this is still prison, we're still in it – it's just a fraction wider, that's all. These trees, the hedges, merely serve to mask the walls.

MARY. Then thank God for them. Now I can dream – and paint my kingdom as wide as I will. As far as the unfettered eye can see . . . all those clouds scudding through the sky are little ships all sailing off to France. Bon Voyage – say hello to my homeland – be my ambassadors, bear good news. But careful, stay in the air, not a foot on the ground – then you'll never be subject to this cruel queen.

KENNEDY. Freedom has turned your head, my lady.

MARY. Sh. Look over there – a fisherman landing his boat. A poor man. But his leaky vessel would be enough to spirit me away to where my friends are waiting – I'd cram his nets with rubies and sink his little boat – if he would only save me.

KENNEDY. Don't you see the black horsemen riding over there? Driving everyone away, both friends and foes – that fisherman is probably a spy.

MARY. No, dear Hanna. This is all meant. All part of a greater plan. This chink of happiness can only lead to brighter things. Believe me, the hand of love has played a part in this and that hand belongs to Leicester's mighty arm. And bit by bit, my prison walls will widen and widen, and more and more light will pour in – until the day that it's all sunlight and space –

and I'll see his face – and on that day all my chains will simply
fall away.

KENNEDY. Yesterday you heard you were condemned to death,
today you dream only of freedom. I can't keep up with you.

MARY. Quiet. Can you hear the hunting horns, calling me over
the hills. Oh God, if I had a black stallion I'd race him through
the fields and join the hunt and gallop far away as I used to.
You hear that sweet, sad haloo-ing? . . . drawing me home, to
my girlhood, back to France.

Act Three Scene Two

Enter PAULET.

PAULET. Well, my lady. I think you'll agree I've done something
right at last. I trust you're grateful.

MARY. Sir. Did you do this for me? You!

PAULET. And why not me? I delivered your letter. As I promised.

MARY. You delivered it? – and this sudden burst of freedom came
from that little letter . . .

PAULET (*pointedly*). Yes indeed – and there's better to come –
even greater things than this . . .

MARY. What do you mean?

PAULET. You hear the horns?

MARY. Yes – what? You frighten me.

PAULET. The Queen, Her Royal Majesty, is hunting nearby.

MARY. What?

PAULET. And soon she'll be here – before your eyes.

MARY *swoons visibly.*

KENNEDY. My lady, you look pale.

PAULET. What's the matter with her? Isn't this what she wanted?
Sooner perhaps than expected – but nonetheless.

MARY. Why did no-one warn me? I'm not ready for it, not now –
the thing I dreamed of most rears up and threatens to crush me
– I can't bear it, I can't bear it. Quick Hanna, back inside – I
must compose myself . . .

PAULET. Stay where you are.

Act Three Scene Three

Enter TALBOT.

MARY. Lord Talbot – my former jailer – and my kindest. Please, I
can't see her, I won't see her, don't make me.

TALBOT. Pull yourself together. This is the moment of truth.

MARY. I've rehearsed this a thousand times in my thoughts, how
I'd move her with the story of my woes, but now I don't know
what to say . . . I've forgotten. The sea of honeyed words has
drained away, revealing the zigzag rocks of hatred – that's all I
can feel. Pure, black, shining hatred – and all my good
intentions have deserted me.

TALBOT. Fight it. Fight your anger. Nothing good can come of it
when hatred meets hatred head on. Swallow everything – she
has the power – you must abase yourself.

MARY. What? To her? Never.

TALBOT. You must. Speak to her with deference – speak to her
heart – don't mention justice nor your claim. That must wait till
the ground has been laid.

MARY. We never should have met like this. No good can come of
this; the marriage of fire and water, the embrace of the lion and
the lamb – she's driven me too far, and I've been hurt too deep
– there can be no reconciliation between us. None.

TALBOT. Of course. Of course. But see her first. My lady, she's
not devoid of feeling. Her eyes welled up when she read your
letter. I saw her. Deep in her soul she's looking for
appeasement, which is why I came ahead – to be sure you were
calm in your mind.

MARY. Is Burleigh there, my angel of death?

TALBOT. No-one's with her but the Earl of Leicester.

MARY. Lord Leicester!

TALBOT. You mustn't be afraid of him. He isn't plotting your downfall. Indeed, he bent the Queen's will to this meeting.

MARY. I knew it.

TALBOT. I'm sorry?

PAULET. She's coming.

Act Three Scene Four

They move aside. MARY *remains, leaning against her nurse. Enter* ELIZABETH, LEICESTER, *followers.*

ELIZABETH. What place is this? (*To* LEICESTER.)

LEICESTER. It's Fotheringay your Majesty.

ELIZABETH. Have the whole hunt sent back to London – too many people. Let us seek some peace and quiet here.

TALBOT *sends the followers away:* THE QUEEN *looks at* MARY, *but still speaks to* PAULET.

My people are sometimes overfond. Fanatical almost. Almost idolatrous. As if I were a goddess, not a Queen.

MARY (*stands up straight – looks straight at* ELIZABETH, *shudders and reaches for her nurse again*). God help me. That is a face that hasn't got a heart.

ELIZABETH. Who is this lady?

Silence.

LEICESTER. Majesty, you're in Fotheringay.

ELIZABETH (*feigns surprise and horror – and turns darkly to* LEICESTER). Have you done this, Lord Leicester?

LEICESTER. It has happened Majesty; and now that Heaven has led you here; I pray charity and mercy may prevail.

TALBOT. Please, Majesty, cast your royal eyes on this wretched woman trembling before you.

MARY *summons up her strength, and goes to* ELIZABETH
but cannot. Merely stands and stares at her, unable to speak.

ELIZABETH. Excuse me my Lord – was I not told she was a
broken woman – this one is proud, her head held high, and
doesn't seem too troubled by remorse.

MARY. Very well. One more bitter draught for me to swallow.
Farewell pride, pointless pride – let me forget who I am, forget
what I've suffered, and grovel before the author of my misery.

(*To* ELIZABETH.). Heaven is on your side, cousin. The victory
is yours. So let me worship the God who plainly worships you.

She falls at her feet.

And now, dear cousin, show your true nobility of spirit; do not
leave me to languish here, stretch out your royal hand – for I
have fallen so far that only you can pull me from the mire.

ELIZABETH (*withdrawing*). That is your rightful place, and I
thank my merciful God in Heaven that I am not where you are
now.

MARY. Well then. Remember this – fortune is capricious and
most changeable. There are Gods who punish pride and
arrogance. If you respect me then you respect yourself. By
insulting me, you insult the Tudor blood which binds us both.
How can you stand there, cold and hard, like a rocky cliff, sheer
and inaccessible to the shipwrecked soul, who's desperate for
land? Everything I have and am, my life, my hopes, all depend
on your favour. And on the power of my hot tears to melt your
heart. But you are like a basilisk of ice – you freeze my tears
and turn my heart to stone. And my sad words are stuck in my
throat.

ELIZABETH. Get to the point, my Lady Stuart. You wished to
speak with me. Well here I am. So, speak. I have a duty, I'll
admit it, as a sister to hear you out in sorrow and in sympathy.
There are those who say that no dialogue is thinkable with the
agents of Terror. And you won't deny that you have tried to
have me killed.

MARY. How to begin? God must help me to perfume my words.
Roses, not thorns. It's hard to plead my case without accusing
you of outrage – and I mustn't. Even so you have used me most
unjustly – for I am – as you know – a Queen – as you are – and
you have treated me like a common criminal. I came here a
suppliant, and you – scorning all your laws and all my rights –

confined me in a dungeon, ripped away, most viciously, my
friends, my servants. I was ignominiously deprived and
shamed, and dragged before some clapboard court, on a
trumped-up charge, condemned – but enough of that. I must,
today, draw a veil over everything you made me suffer. So let's
rather call it a twist of fate. You're not to blame – I'm not to
blame. Fate. It is the fate of Kings, that their disputes will rend
the world in half – and from the dark split the furies, soaked in
hatred, scuttle out and infect us all.

Good. Now we needn't talk as strangers any more. Now we
stand face to face, as sisters. So speak to me as a sister. Tell me
what I've done. Say what you will. My God. If only you had
listened to me then, in my hour of need. Then it wouldn't have
come to this, and we wouldn't be holding this sad meeting in
this sad, sad place.

ELIZABETH. Thank God my guardian angel saved me from
nursing such an adder at my breast. A twist of fate you say?
Not at all. Rather the black hatred of your black heart. And the
naked ambition of the Stuarts. But God is on my side, not
yours. And that is why my head is safe and strong. And why
yours must fall.

MARY. My life is in God's hands – I don't believe you would
abuse your own power – not so bloodily.

ELIZABETH. Oh? Why shouldn't I? Who's going to stop me?
Your uncle shows the world how enemies should be treated. St.
Bartholomew's Day was a lesson to us all. Ties of blood,
international law, excuse me, what's all that to me, when the
church can undo any treaty, when it sanctifies the killing of
kings. No, I'll only practise what your priests have taught me.
What security can you offer me if I were fool enough to set you
free? What padlock could safeguard your loyalty which St.
Peter couldn't pick open with his skeleton keys. Force is the
only security and I'll not forge treaties with a nest of vipers.

MARY. You see. You've always looked on me as an enemy, as an
alien. If you'd but named me as your heiress, as was my due,
then you'd see nothing in my heart but gratitude and love, from
a kinswoman and from a friend.

ELIZABETH. Your only kin are papists overseas – your only
friends are renegades and monks. What? Name you my heir?
Fall into that trap? You wouldn't even wait until I died; as I live
you're still trying to seduce my people, a latter-day Circe,

trying to entrap the noblest of young England, in your harlot's
net, and turning them to beasts . . .

MARY. Listen. Rule in peace. Do what you will. I hereby
renounce all claims to your dominions. My God. You see, my
spirit has been hamstrung by despair – I've no ambition any
more. You've won. I'm Mary's shadow. Nobility quietly
broken behind bars. You've done your worst, my very blood,
my sap's contaminated. You've destroyed me in my bloom. So
please, say the word. Say what I know you came to say. I can't
believe you came all this way merely to mock your victim. Say
it – say, 'Mary, you are free. You have tasted my power, now
taste my mercy'. You've but to say it and give me back my
freedom and my life. One word can undo everything you've
done. I long to hear it. Don't make me wait for ever. Say it.
And if you don't – well, beware. For, sister – I would not, for
all the kingdoms in the world, stand there before you as you
stand before me.

ELIZABETH. Oh, so now at last we admit defeat, do we? What's
the matter? No more schemes afoot? No more secret murderers
on the warpath? No more rash young knights to fight your
cause? No – nothing. It's all over. No-one left to seduce!
Shame! The world's forgotten you – there're no more
candidates for the dubious honour of being your fourth husband
– and not surprising since you seem to kill your suitors as
efficiently as you kill your husbands.

MARY. Sister how dare you! God, grant me patience!

ELIZABETH. Look, Lord Leicester. Look at the charms that no
man can gaze upon with impunity, next to which all
womankind's supposed to pale. That reputation has been
cheaply bought, I see. This beauty which is so commonly
admired, is plainly admired merely as common property.

MARY. This is too much.

ELIZABETH (*laughing scornfully*). And now we see the real face.
Quite unmasked.

MARY. I made mistakes. But I was only human
And young. And power seduced me. That I never
Have denied, nor sought to hide my faults
I have confessed them – as befits a Queen.
The world knows all the worst of me, and yet
I know I'm better than my reputation.
But woe betide you if the world should ever

Remove the cloak of honour from your deeds
And show them as they are, all black and sinful,
Hate and lust combined – it's in the blood,
We know your virtues on your mother's side,
We all know why it was that Anne Boleyn
Mounted the scaffold.

TALBOT. Has it come to this?
God in Heaven, Lady Mary, is this forbearance, is this
submission?

MARY. Forbearance? I have born as much as anyone
Can bear, and now it is enough! Enough
Of lily-livered patience, pale submission
Now it's time
For anger, red and raw, to burst its banks,
To let my tongue and all my hatred smear
Your face with blood and venom.

TALBOT. She's gone mad.
Her sorrows are too much for her, forgive her.

ELIZABETH *is speechless.* LEICESTER *tries to lead her
away.*

LEICESTER. Come away, quickly, from this accursed place.

MARY. England's throne has been profaned by a bastard Queen.
This noble land tricked by an imposter. If there was any justice
you'd be on your knees, grovelling before me in the dirt, for
I'm your rightful Queen – and you know it.

ELIZABETH *rushes off, the Lords follow.*

Act Three Scene Five

KENNEDY. What have you done? – now it's over, all our hope is
dead.

MARY (*still possessed*). At last, at last Hanna, after all these years
of degradation, one golden moment of triumph and revenge,
and oh, the weight fallen from my shoulders – the weight of
mountains – to think, I had a dagger in my hand and I plunged
it in her heart.

KENNEDY. You're mad, you're mad. Can't you see? She's the
Queen. She forges thunderbolts and you humiliated her in front
of all her favourites.

MARY. Yes, in front of Leicester. I did. He saw it, he witnessed
my triumph. And I toppled her from her pedestal – he was there
– I could feel his strength, urging me onward . . .

Act Three Scene Six

Enter MORTIMER.

KENNEDY. Oh Sir, this is disaster . . .

MORTIMER. I heard everything.

He sends KENNEDY *away.*

I heard you demolish her and grind her to the dust. You were
the Queen and she the common criminal. Such courage! You
are a goddess, let me worship you.

MARY. Did you speak with Lord Leicester? Did you give him my
letter, tell me, quickly Sir.

MORTIMER. Such noble anger, flashing about you like summer
lightning – you are the most beautiful woman on God's earth.

MARY. No, tell me, tell me, what did he say? What should I hope
for?

MORTIMER. Hope? From him? He's just a coward, no hope from
that quarter – quite despicable, forget him!

MARY. What?

MORTIMER. Him, rescue you? Claim you? Let him try – he'll
have to reckon with me first and to the death.

MARY. So you didn't give him my letter? Then I'm done for.

MORTIMER. He's much too much in love with life to help you.
The man who saves you has to embrace death as a friend.

MARY. What can you do?

MORTIMER. Things have changed. Things have gone too far.
You saw the Queen when she left you. There's no hope of

mercy. None at all. We must take action – we must strike now
or never and you must be free by morning.

MARY. Tonight? It can't be done.

MORTIMER. Listen. My friends are gathered nearby – a priest
heard our confession and granted us absolution in advance. And
so our path to glory is prepared.

MARY. Oh God.

MORTIMER. We storm the castle tonight. The keys are ours. We
will kill the guards then steal you away – we can't leave
witnesses, everyone here must die.

MARY. Your uncle?

MORTIMER. My uncle first of all. I'll kill him myself.

MARY. Sin upon sin!

MORTIMER. I told you, all our future sins are forgiven. I'm free
to do my worst, and by God I will.

MARY. God help us.

MORTIMER. And if I have to stab the Queen to death then I'll do
it – I've sworn it on the Bible.

MARY. No, Mortimer. Too much blood.

MORTIMER. What is life compared to you and my love for you?
Let the bonds of the world burst apart, let a second flood sweep
all humanity from the earth – let the whole universe collapse
but never let me turn my back on you.

MARY. God in Heaven. Mad, whirling words. Mad, staring eyes.
God, you terrify me.

MORTIMER (*calm*). Why? Life's just a little moment. And
death's another. So – let them drag me bodily to Tyburn –
pluck me limb from limb with red hot irons – if only I can hold
you in my arms . . .

MARY. Get back, how dare you.

MORTIMER. Hold you tight and press my loving mouth . . .

MARY. Let me go, let me go back in.

MORTIMER . You're given me by God; I'll rescue you. I swear
it by the living God and by that God I swear that I'll possess
you too.

MARY. Is there no God to protect me now? From despair to misery to danger! Have hate and love conspired to rule my life?

MORTIMER. They have. For as those men hate you – incandescently – so I love you. They want to sever this soft white neck. So my lady, offer up to the God of Love what they would sacrifice on the altar of hate. Your body's forfeit unto death, so let me use it now. Your hair, soft as silk, is already stamped the property of death. So let your slave drown himself in it.

MARY. Respect my grief, Sir, if not my rank.

MORTIMER. You have no rank – no crown, no earthly majesty. Nothing is left but your heavenly beauty. And for that I would venture everything, it draws me to the headsman's axe and beyond.

MARY. You're mad. Who can save me now?

MORTIMER. A brave deed deserves a brave reward. Only a madman would shed his blood for nothing. The only purpose of life is to live it. So let me feel the heat of your breast, as hot as mine.

MARY. Who can save me . . . from my own saviour?

MORTIMER. Don't pretend. You're not cold. The whole world knows you're slippery and open to the urgency of love. You pleasured Rizzio, they say, is that not right? And Bothwell had the freedom of you.

MARY. Shameless!

MORTIMER. He was your master, you trembled before him and you loved it. It's fear that thrills you – I won't disappoint you. I'll show you fear. I'll make you beg for mercy.

KENNEDY (*running in*). Quick, danger, danger. Armed men everywhere. Surrounding us.

MORTIMER. I'll protect you

MARY. Hanna. Save me. Where can I run to? Who can I turn to?

They flee inside.

Act Three Scene Seven

PAULET *enters, his followers rush across the stage.*

PAULET. Shut the gates.

MORTIMER. Uncle, what is it?

PAULET. Where's the murderess? Lock her up.

MORTIMER. What's happened?

PAULET. The Queen. Blasphemy, treason – foul treason.

MORTIMER. The Queen, which Queen?

PAULET. The Queen of England. She's been murdered on the road to London.

Exit.

Act Three Scene Eight

Enter O'KELLY.

MORTIMER. Can I believe my ears? Did someone say the Queen was murdered? O'Kelly, what's happened, what's wrong, man?

O'RELLY. Run Mortimer, all is lost.

MORTIMER. What's lost?

O'KELLY. No questions, go, quickly!

MORTIMER. What's happened?

O'KELLY. It was Sauvage, he did it. Bloody madman.

MORTIMER. So it's true?

O'KELLY. It's true – quick, go!

MORTIMER. She's murdered then? And Mary can be Queen?

O'KELLY. Murdered? What d'you mean?

MORTIMER. You said . . .

O'KELLY. She's alive. And we are dead.

MORTIMER. Alive . . .

O'KELLY. The blow fell wide of the mark. Her cloak protected her. Talbot disarmed him.

MORTIMER. Alive . . .

O'KELLY. Alive to kill us all. Quick, they'll have the park surrounded . . .

MORTIMER. Who was it?

O'KELLY. Sauvage – selfish idiot. He'd planned it all with our priest – to free our church with one fell swoop. Martyrdom and glory. Madness. Will you come with me?

MORTIMER. No, go alone and may God protect you.

O'KELLY *exits.*

I'll stay here – I've one last chance to save
My Queen – or we will share a common grave.

MORTIMER *exits.*

Act Four Scene One

An antechamber. AUBESPINE, KENT, LEICESTER.

AUBESPINE. How is her Majesty? My Lords, I've just heard the news – I'm amazed – how could it happen, when she was surrounded by her people?

LEICESTER. It happened, Monsieur, because it was not one of her people but one of yours . . .

AUBESPINE. A madman, I'm certain.

KENT. A papist, Monsieur Le Comte.

Enter BURLEIGH, *talking to* DAVISON.

BURLEIGH. Have the death warrant drawn up – as soon as possible. Prepare the seal and bring it to the Queen to sign. Quickly.

DAVISON. Very good, sir.

Exit.

AUBESPINE. My Lord – my loyal heart rejoices that Heaven has protected your revered Queen from this vicious attack.

BURLEIGH. Heaven protected her from her enemies.

AUBESPINE. May God curse the man who did it.

BURLEIGH. Amen. And those who urged him to it.

AUBESPINE (*to* KENT). Lord Marshal, will you lead me to the Queen and let me assure her of my Lord and master's warmest good wishes.

BURLEIGH. Don't trouble yourself, Monsieur le Comte.

AUBESPINE. No trouble, I assure you. I'm quite aware of what I should do.

BURLEIGH. The only thing you should do, Monsieur, is to leave this island as quickly as possible.

AUBESPINE. I beg your pardon?

BURLEIGH. You have protection for today – but tomorrow it expires.

AUBESPINE. What is my crime?

BURLEIGH. Better not to name it . . . it would never be forgiven.

AUBESPINE. But my diplomatic immunity . . .

BURLEIGH. Not applicable to traitors.

LEICESTER/KENT. What?

AUBESPINE. Consider well what you are saying.

BURLEIGH. A free pass, signed by your hand, was found in the assassin's pocket.

KENT. Impossible!

AUBESPINE. I sign many such passes, I can't see into the hearts of all the recipients.

BURLEIGH. He said his last confession in your house.

AUBESPINE. My house is open.

BURLEIGH. Plainly open to all of England's enemies.

AUBESPINE. I demand an investigation.

BURLEIGH. I wouldn't if I were you.

AUBESPINE. I represent the King – you insult him in my person – beware; he will tear the marriage treaty into a hundred pieces.

BURLEIGH. The Queen has saved him the trouble. England will not be allied to France. My Lord of Kent – give these gentlemen safe-conduct to the coast. The mob has already stormed his palace, and uncovered his secret arsenal. They are threatening to tear him apart – so you'd better keep him hidden for his own safety. Guard him well.

AUBESPINE. I'll be glad to leave this accursed nation, where international law is held in contempt and where treaties are valued as old playbills. But my King will call you to account – and bloodily . . .

BURLEIGH. Let him try!

KENT *and* AUBESPINE *exeunt.*

Act Four Scene Two

LEICESTER. So now you must unpick the knot you took such pains to tie. Nobody desired it but you, not a soul in England. Couldn't you have saved yourself the trouble?

BURLEIGH. My intentions were of the best. But God decreed otherwise. I have nothing on my conscience – perhaps not everyone can say as much!

LEICESTER. Lord Burleigh is in his element once more. I know that dark, unflinching look – we're on the hunt for traitors once again. It's the perfect time for you – a crime's been committed, but the facts are still a little vague. So – inquisitions now, I think, and purges. A word, a look, anything's indictable now – men's very thoughts will be dragged before the court. And you are the man of the moment, the nation's Atlas, all England on your shoulders.

BURLEIGH. As far as statecraft and intrigue are concerned, I bow to you, the master Machiavell.

LEICESTER. What do you mean, my Lord?

BURLEIGH. You managed to lure the Queen to Fotheringay Castle – and all behind my back.

LEICESTER. Behind your back? Excuse me, sir, but what would I have to hide from you?

BURLEIGH (*with heavy irony*). Oh, I see, you mean the Queen led you to Fotheringay – out of the kindness of her heart?

LEICESTER. I'm sorry, what are you trying to say?

BURLEIGH. It certainly explains the course of moderation you were proposing in council. And of course poor Mary Stuart; such a weak and broken woman, no match for the Queen, hardly worth the effort, certainly not the risk of shedding her blood – very cleverly argued.

LEICESTER. This is slander. Come with me straight away and explain yourself before her Royal Highness.

BURLEIGH. Gladly. And good luck. You'll need every scrap of eloquence you have.

Exit.

LEICESTER. I'm discovered – the wretch can see right through me. But how did he find out? If he has any concrete proof, then God help me. And if Elizabeth finds out about my understanding with the Queen of Scots, then I would be steeped in guilt from top to toe. How cunning my advice would seem in retrospect, all the pains I took to lure her to Fotheringay, it would look like manifest betrayal. She'd never, ever forgive me – because now, of course, it all looks planned – her humiliation, everything. Even the attack on her, which was just a trick of fate. But the trick will look like mine – and nothing will save me.

Enter MORTIMER.

MORTIMER. Lord Leicester, are we alone?

LEICESTER. Get out, you fool, what do you want here?

MORTIMER. They're on our trail, yours as well.

LEICESTER. Get out!

MORTIMER. They know that there were private meetings at Aubespine's palace . . .

LEICESTER. What's that to me?

MORTIMER. And that the assassin . . .

LEICESTER. Look – all this is your business, not mine. How dare you implicate me in your desperate affairs? *Your* crimes, *your* bloodshed, you defend yourself.

MORTIMER. You must listen to me.

LEICESTER. You can go to Hell. I'll have no truck with common cut-throats.

MORTIMER. You're not listening – I've come to warn you – they're after you as well.

LEICESTER. Nonsense!

MORTIMER. It's true. Burleigh was at Fotheringay. He had the Queen's chambers searched from top to bottom and he found . . .

LEICESTER. Found what?

MORTIMER. A draft of a letter from our Queen – to you.

LEICESTER. My God. Poor woman.

MORTIMER. In which she implores you to keep your word, renews the promise of her hand – and even refers to the picture she sent you . . .

LEICESTER. Death and damnation.

MORTIMER. And now Burleigh has that letter.

LEICESTER. Then I'm dead.

MORTIMER. Listen, seize the moment. Act quickly, save yourself, save her. Invent a thousand stories, avert the worst. Do what you can; I can do no more . . . My comrades have been scattered, our confederacy blown apart. I'm for Scotland, I'll rally new friends there. Now it's your turn, do your best – do it quickly. Do something – do it now.

LEICESTER. You're absolutely right. I will.

Goes to the door.

Guards! Seize this man! And guard him close. He's a traitor – a conspiracy has been unmasked, and he's at its heart. I'll tell the Queen myself.

He exits.

MORTIMER. Villain. Traitor. Double traitor. My fall has become a bridge for his escape. So be it – save your measly life – I'll not say a word – even in death.

The officer of the watch tries to bind him.

And what do you want, slave? You're in chains and I am free.

He draws a knife.

OFFICER. Watch him – he's armed.

They attack him, he defends himself.

MORTIMER. You've sold yourselves to a usurping bastard Queen.

OFFICER. Shut his mouth – seize him.

MORTIMER. My beloved Lady. I couldn't set you free, but I can still show you how to die. Mary, holy Mary pray for me and be mine in the life to come . . .

He stabs himself. Falls.

Act Four Scene Three

QUEEN ELIZABETH's *apartments*. BURLEIGH *and*
ELIZABETH.

ELIZABETH. The traitor. How dare he mock me like that – how
dare he parade me in triumph before his paramour. No woman's
ever suffered so disgracefully.

BURLEIGH. I hope that now you understand my caution.

ELIZABETH. I didn't heed your counsel – and look at me, I'm
punished for it now. I made him the greatest of the great and let
him behave at court as if he were King.

BURLEIGH. And all that time he was deceiving you – with the
Queen of Scotland.

ELIZABETH. She'll pay for that – in blood. Is the death-warrant
ready?

BURLEIGH. It's drawn up as you commanded.

ELIZABETH. Then she will die.
    And he will see her die, then die himself.
    Already I've expunged him from my heart.
    Love's been banished – now revenge and hate
    Have been sucked in to take its place -
    And I promise you his fall will be as abject
    As his rank was great . . .
    So take him to the Tower – and let me choose
    The peers to judge him. Let him feel the full
    And fearsome rigour of the law.

BURLEIGH. He'll try and win you round, beware, he'll try to
justify his treachery.

ELIZABETH. I won't grant him access. Never again. Have you
given the orders?

BURLEIGH. Indeed I have. His entrance will be barred. Depend
upon it.

PAGE (*rushing on*). The Earl of Leicester!

ELIZABETH. What? I won't see him – tell him I won't see him.

PAGE. I couldn't tell his Lordship that. Nor would he believe me
if I did.

ELIZABETH. Is this why I raised him to glory – so my servants
would fear him more than me?

BURLEIGH. The Queen refuses him admission, tell him that. At once.

The PAGE *exits uncertainly.*

ELIZABETH. But what if he could justify his action? What if there were some perfectly obvious . . . I mean, it could be a trick of Mary's to separate me from my dearest friend – she's a slippery piece, a vixen, there's nothing she wouldn't . . .

BURLEIGH. Um, your majesty, really in all conscience . . .

Act Four Scene Four

LEICESTER *bursts in followed by embarrassed servants.*

LEICESTER. Where is the man who dares deny me access to my Queen?

ELIZABETH. How dare you?

LEICESTER. What, turn me away? If you can be seen by Lord Burleigh, you can be seen by me.

BURLEIGH. You are bold, sir. To burst in here without permission.

LEICESTER. And you, sir, are impertinent. Permission! No-one at this court gives the Earl of Leicester permission, nor refuses it – and I will hear it only from my sweet Queen's mouth.

ELIZABETH. Out of my sight, Bastard.

LEICESTER. That isn't my Elizabeth's true voice. This noble Lord is using it for his own ends. My enemy is speaking, but not you. I appeal to you, my Elizabeth. You've listened to him – do I not deserve as much.

ELIZABETH. Speak then – do your worst! Deny your crimes, if you dare and so add perjury to their number.

LEICESTER. First dismiss this popinjay – yes, off you go my Lord – what I have to say to my Queen requires no outside witnesses. Go!

ELIZABETH. No, stay. I order you to stay.

LEICESTER. I've no desire to talk to standers-by! This is a matter for my sovereign and myself. I demand the right due to my rank. He must go. He must. I will need no more than two moments before we are as one.

ELIZABETH. You can't talk me round so easily.

LEICESTER. No, you're absolutely right – I don't have Burleigh's way with words, I'll just try in my simple way to talk to your heart.

ELIZABETH. You are condemned out of hand. My Lord, show him the letter . . .

BURLEIGH. Here it is . . .

LEICESTER. This is the Stuart woman's handwriting.

ELIZABETH. Read it.

LEICESTER (*reads – then calmly*). Appearances are indeed against me. But I trust I will not be judged according to appearances.

ELIZABETH. Can you deny that you were in secret league with her – that you received letters, and her portrait, and led her to believe, to hope she might be free.

LEICESTER. It would be very simple, if I were guilty to deny everything. To say this is all a pack of lies. However my conscience is quite clear – so I can say that what she writes is true in every particular.

ELIZABETH. Well then.

BURLEIGH. Damned by his own confession.

ELIZABETH. Out of my sight. Lock him up. You traitor!

LEICESTER. I am no traitor. My only fault was not to make my actions clear to you. It was done in secret – wrongly, as I now perceive, but for the right reason. My aim was to smoke your enemy out and thus to be certain of her downfall.

ELIZABETH. Pathetic!

BURLEIGH. Lord Leicester, do you really think . . .

LEICESTER. Yes, I know – it was a dangerous game – which no-one else at court could dare to play. The whole world knows how I execrate the Stuart woman and everything she stands for. Only a man at the pinnacle of your favour could dare to act alone, in order to do his duty, to do good.

BURLEIGH. If the deed were so good, why shroud it in secrecy?

LEICESTER. My dear Lord Burleigh, we all know it is your custom to tell us all what you're about to do before you do it. You are the bell of your own actions, clamouring them abroad before they're done. Well, fair enough, that's your way. Mine is to act first and talk afterwards.

BURLEIGH. You're only talking now because you have to.

LEICESTER. And you think you've performed the most amazing feat of derring-do, saved your Queen, brought treachery to light – you flatter yourself that nothing escapes your beady eye – all swagger and vanity. In spite of all your spies – were it not for me Mary Stuart would be free today.

BURLEIGH. You sir?

LEICESTER. None other. The queen confided in Mortimer. She, perhaps unwisely, opened her soul to him. She went further, she sent him on a secret, bloody mission directed against Mary, a mission that his uncle had previously refused . . . Tell me, is this true or not. Well, which?

BURLEIGH. What on earth makes you think the Queen would ever . . .

LEICESTER. Is it true? It's not denied, I see. And where were your thousand eyes, my Lord; they couldn't see that Mortimer was a traitor, a renegade, a papist tool, Mary Stuart's puppet, a wild and unrepentant fanatic, come to these shores with the express purpose of freeing Mary and murdering the Queen . . .

ELIZABETH. My Mortimer?

LEICESTER. The same. I was the go-between between Mary and himself, that's how I found him out. And today she was to be snatched from prison. He told me so himself. Just now he told me. I ordered his arrest and in despair that he was thwarted and unmasked, he took his life.

ELIZABETH. How I have been deceived. My Mortimer.

BURLEIGH. And this happened when? Just now – just after I left you?

LEICESTER. Yes. It is most regrettable. His testimony would have cleared my name.

BURLEIGH. He killed himself, you say. Are you sure you didn't help him on his way?

LEICESTER. That isn't worthy of you. Bring the watch here.

He goes to the door and summons the captain of the guard.

Tell Her Majesty how Mortimer died.

OFFICER. I was waiting outside when his Lordship suddenly appeared. He told me to arrest Lord Mortimer as a traitor – that Mortimer screamed in rage – drew his dagger and, saving your presence – cursed the Queen to damnation and, before we could stop him, stabbed himself. He was dead before he hit the ground. And then –

LEICESTER. Thank you. That will do. The Queen knows enough.

Exit CAPTAIN.

ELIZABETH. Monstrous treachery.

LEICESTER. So your Majesty, who was it saved you? Was it Lord Burleigh. Did he even know you were in danger? No, Leicester was your only guardian angel.

BURLEIGH. This Mortimer died most conveniently for you, Lord Leicester.

ELIZABETH. I don't know what to say. I believe you and I don't. You're plainly guilty, but just as plainly not. That damned woman – all this is because of her.

LEICESTER. And she must die. Yes, I see that now. I said before that you should stay your hand until she sinned against you. Now she has – so strike her down. Carry out your sentence.

BURLEIGH. You said what, sir? What was your advice?

LEICESTER. I can see that this bloody sacrifice is necessary to safeguard the Queen. Therefore let the death warrant be drawn up – and as quickly as possible.

BURLEIGH. Since his Lordship shows such devotion and such zeal, may I suggest that he supervises the execution. Personally, I mean. What better way to dispel any lingering suspicion hanging over you, than that you see to it, see in person that that fair head, which once – or so your enemies insist – you loved – be struck off.

ELIZABETH. This is excellent advice. Let it be so.

LEICESTER. I would have thought my rank exempted me from such sordid duties. It's surely more Lord Burleigh's sort of thing. But yes, of course, to prove my devotion to my Queen,

I gladly waive the privilege of rank and willingly agree to undertake this duty, repellent though it is.

ELIZABETH. Good. Lord Burleigh will assist you.
(*To* BURLEIGH). See that the warrant is drawn up, immediately.

BURLEIGH *exits. Noise without.*

Enter KENT.

KENT. My Lady, there's uproar in the streets. The mob is clamouring for you, demands to see your face.

ELIZABETH. What do they want?

KENT. They want to know their sovereign isn't dead. They want Mary Stuart's head – to see her die today. Only that will appease them.

ELIZABETH. So they are to force my hand?

KENT. It will be hard to dissuade them . . .

Act Four Scene Five

TALBOT *enters.* KENT *goes to look out of a window.*

TALBOT. Majesty, don't let them force you to a rash decision – be firm, be resolute.

He notices DAVISON *holding the paper.*

Or has it happened already? What is that paper in your hand – no, the Queen mustn't see it.

ELIZABETH. Lord Talbot, they're forcing me –

TALBOT. Who can force you? Who would dare? You must assert your majesty – silence these roaring boys. The mob is angry, terror stalks the streets – you're only human, too distraught to formulate a proper judgement.

BURLEIGH. That judgement has been made already. The sentence has been passed. Now it's merely a question of carrying it out. Nothing else.

KENT (*returning*). We can't keep them back much longer . . .

ELIZABETH. You see my Lord, they are, they're forcing me.

TALBOT. Just stop and think. A single word can mean so much.
Wait until your mind's your own – wait until a calmer time than
this.

BURLEIGH. Yes, that's right, wait until your Kingdom is in
flames, till your enemies have mown you down.

TALBOT. I'm not going to speak to you of justice. But think of
this. You're afraid of Mary now – while she's alive. But it's the
dead, decapitated Mary that you should fear the most. She will
rise from her tomb, the grizzly spirit of revenge, and stalk your
kingdom sowing rebellion and death. Your people hate her only
because they fear her, when she is no more they will avenge
her. When she's dead you'll see another England – for when
we murder her we murder Justice. Tyranny will stalk the land.
You'll process through utter devastation – like Boadicea
through a battlefield – no cheering crowds, no crowds at all –
pure terror, hanging like a plague over England.

ELIZABETH. Talbot. Today you saved my life. I thank you, but
now I wish to God you'd let him strike me down. Then I would
lie at peace inside my grave and be spared this torment, this tug
of war, this doubt, this blame, this heavy duty.
My God, I swear to you
I'm weary of this life and of this crown.
If one of us must die to save the other –
And it is clear there is no other way –
Then God let it be me. I surrender.
My people must decide – I give them back
The sovereignty which they gave to me.
God is my witness that I always strove
For them – not for myself. And if they think
This callow queen, this flatterer, this Stuart
Would rule them better – well then let her rule,
I was never meant to reign. I see it now –
It needs a heart of iron – mine's too soft,
That's all.

BURLEIGH. You claim to love your people above yourself. Then
prove it, for God's sake. How can you opt for peace and quiet
for your own heart and death and disarray for the rest of
England. Think of the church, of how this woman would
haul us back to the dark ages. And re-instate the monks and
welcome back the prelates and the pope of Rome, destroy our

churches – dethrone our Kings. Not just your subjects, but their immortal souls – whether they are saved or damned – all this depends on you. It's not the time for milk-and-water clemency. You have one duty, only one; to your people and their welfare. Talbot saved your life – and we all thank him for that – but let me save your kingdom. That is greater.

ELIZABETH. Just leave me to my thoughts. You can no longer help me. I'll put this matter to my God, the greatest judge of all. And as he commands, so I will obey. Leave me now.

ELIZABETH (*to* DAVISON). Stay close at hand.

They all withdraw – TALBOT *last of all, he looks at her reproachfully and anxiously.*

Act Four Scene Six

ELIZABETH. This slavery of service to the people. God, I'm so weary of flattering this idol I despise. When will I be free to reign as I want to reign? And not be forced to grovel for their favour, to fawn upon a mob who'd rather see a Punch and Judy show? Why have I practised justice all my life, and abjured tyranny, why? For what? If the first time that brute force must be deployed my hands are tied? Is justice part of my free will? Hardly. Here I stand, a weak and defenceless woman – myself against the world. Quite naked. For all I try and bedeck myself with justice and with virtue, my enemies' hatred strips me bare, and reveals the blemishes, the shame which my father lent me at my birth. And there I stand – and there she stands, their mascot, their madonna, my waking nightmare, Mary Stuart.

But I can put an end to fear, like that. Simple: her head will fall, I'll be at peace at last. She's the fury of my life, the harpie sent by fate to pluck at me and claw my face. She steals my lover, tears away my bridegroom. All of my misfortunes have Mary Stuart blazoned across them. But what if she were just blown away? – then I'd be free as mountain air.

Silence while she imagines this.

God, how she looked at me. Undiluted scorn. Her eyes would have scorched the earth. But she's quite powerless, you see.

I have all the weapons in the world – I'll strike you down, and then you'll be no more.

She goes to the table, grasps the pen.

Mary Stuart. And now – it's done . . .

She has signed. Then drops the pen in sudden terror. After a silence, she rings the bell.

Act Four Scene Seven

Enter DAVISON.

ELIZABETH. Where are the other Lords?

DAVISON. Gone, your Majesty, to try to call the angry crowds to order. When they saw my Lord Talbot they calmed down, and people started shouting 'That's him, look that's him, the man who saved the Queen. The bravest man in England – hear what he has to say'. And he spoke and they listened and his calm words, strong, persuasive (you know what he's like) showed them that violence was not the way – and they were pacified.

ELIZABETH. The fickle multitude, eh? A feather to each wind that blows. Who'd put their trust in them? Thank you, though, Lord Davison, this is good news. You may go now.

He's at the door by now.

Oh, and here's the paper – you can take it – I'll leave it in your hands.

DAVISON. Your Majesty – your signature. You've decided?

ELIZABETH. It was to be signed – so I signed it. A piece of paper decides nothing, though. A name cannot kill.

DAVISON. But your name on this paper decides everything and kills as surely as a cannonball. This paper orders the High Sheriff to go directly to Fotheringay Castle and to tell the Queen of Scots that she's to die and then, by dawn, to have the deed performed. There's no going back – no delay. When this paper leaves my hands, she's dead.

ELIZABETH. Yes, so it would seem. Well, God has placed a mighty destiny in your hands. You must pray to Him for guidance. I'll leave you to your duty.

She makes as if to go.

DAVISON. No, your Majesty, I beg you, don't go until you've made your wishes clear. I want to obey you to the letter – so, is this right, you've placed this warrant in my hands to see that it's enforced as soon as possible?

ELIZABETH. That's for your own prudence to decide.

DAVISON. Please God forbid. I have no prudence, not in this regard, only obedience. I'm just your servant, I cannot take decisions. The slightest error here, and the Queen would die unjustly, which would be monstrous. Allow me to be a mere instrument, unthinking and unfeeling. Tell me explicitly what should be done with this death warrant.

ELIZABETH. Surely the name says it all . . .

DAVISON. Indeed; but should it be carried out at once?

ELIZABETH. I don't say that – and I shudder to think it.

DAVISON. So you wish me to keep it, until some later time as yet unspecified?

ELIZABETH. On your head be it.

DAVISON. Oh God in Heaven. Please, Majesty, tell me. What do you want?

ELIZABETH. I want an end to this whole wretched bloody business, and not to have to think about it anymore.

DAVISON. All I require is one clear word. Tell me please, what to do with this paper.

ELIZABETH. I've told you – stop pestering me.

DAVISON. Told me? You've told me nothing. Your Majesty, please, you must remember . . .

ELIZABETH. Really, this is unbearable.

DAVISON. Do, please, have patience with me. I haven't been here long – a few months only – I have yet to learn the language of the court and the ways of Kings. I'm a simple man – so please indulge your humble, simple servant, humour my stupidity and tell me, in language that I can understand, what my duty is -

She turns her back.

Then take it back, take it back. It's like a red hot coal in my hands – give it to someone else – this is a terrible business . . .

ELIZABETH. Do what you have to do.

She exits.

Act Four Scene Eight

DAVISON. She's gone – leaving me with this. As bewildered as before. Curse this thing. Should I keep it safe or pass it on?

BURLEIGH *enters.*

Oh Sir, thank God. Thank God you're here. You appointed me to this office. I'd no idea what it entailed – please, please, release me from it now – this is no place for me.

BURLEIGH. You're raving, man. Pull yourself together. Where's the warrant? What were the Queen's orders?

DAVISON. She left me with it, here – and in such anger. And I've no idea what I should do. Please help me, this is torture. Here it is, it's signed.

BURLEIGH. It's what? Give it to me. Now.

DAVISON. I daren't.

BURLEIGH. I beg your pardon.

DAVISON. The Queen didn't make it clear what I was to do . . .

BURLEIGH. What do you mean? She signed it, didn't she? That's clear enough. Now give it to me.

DAVISON. No. I'm supposed to see that it's carried out – and then, to see that it's not – God I've no idea what I am supposed to do.

BURLEIGH. You're to see it's carried out. And this instant. Give it here. If you delay then you are lost.

DAVISON. But I am lost if I do not.

BURLEIGH. Your senses are plainly lost already. You utter imbecile. Get out of my sight!

DAVISON. What are you doing? Stop. God in Heaven, I am done for.

Act Five Part One

Scene as in Act One. HANNA KENNEDY *in deep mourning,*
eyes red from weeping – quite grief stricken – busy at work,
occasionally breaking off to pray. PAULET *and* DRURY *enter,*
also in black. MARY*'s servants enter carrying silver vessels,*
mirrors, paintings and other valuables, filling the room with them.
PAULET *gives* KENNEDY *a jewel box and a paper – plainly an*
inventory of the articles returned. HANNA *looks again at all the*
treasure – again breaks down into silent grief. Enter MELVILLE,
MARY*'s former steward.*

KENNEDY. Melville; I can't believe it. You've come back to us.

MELVILLE. Yes, most faithful lady – I've returned.

KENNEDY. After such a long and painful separation.

MELVILLE. Indeed. And the reunion is no less painful.

KENNEDY. Oh God, I see you've come . . .

MELVILLE. To bid my Queen farewell forever. Yes.

KENNEDY. She's been denied the presence of her loyal friends
for so long – and now they let you back on the day she's to die.
Oh Sir . . . I won't even ask how you are – or tell you how
we've suffered since you were so cruelly torn from us. They'll
be time enough for that – later. Oh, Melville, I never thought
we'd live to see this day.

MELVILLE. Please Hanna, we have to be strong for each other.
There will be a time for tears – the rest of my life. But
meanwhile, let's be brave. Let others give in to grief – we'll be
a firm prop for her as she walks the road to death.

KENNEDY. Dear Melville – she doesn't need support from you or
me. On the contrary her strength, her composure are an
example to us all. Mary Stuart will go to her death every inch a
queen.

MELVILLE. How did she respond to the decree? She can't have
been ready in her mind.

KENNEDY. She wasn't. We were both expecting to be freed.
Mortimer had promised to lead us from here by morning. So
we waited – the Queen agonising over whether she should
entrust her person and her honour to that hot-headed boy.
Then suddenly we heard a commotion in the castle, a hollow
knocking, loud hammer blows. We thought our liberation had
begun, our spirits soared – the door flew open . . . and it was
Paulet, our jailer, and he told us what the noise was. They were
building a scaffold in the great hall below.

MELVILLE. God in Heaven. How did Queen Mary take all this?

KENNEDY. I saw her cast all earthly hopes aside
And almost smile. As if unburdened. Full
Of faith and strength she turned her face to Heaven.
Not a word or complaint, not a shudder
Not a sigh disgraced my lady's hearing of it.
It was only when she was told of Lord Leicester's shameful
treachery, and that poor Mortimer had met his death for her and
saw how his uncle grieved to lose the last and sweetest hope of
his old age and all because of her – only then did tears begin to
flow. And then they were unstoppable. Not for herself, you
understand, but for all the others she'd damaged.

MELVILLE. Where is she now?

KENNEDY. She spent the rest of the night in prayer, writing
letters of farewell, and writing her will. She's sleeping now.
She needs rest.

MELVILLE. Who's with her?

KENNEDY. Her waiting women all returned to her from London
and her Physician Burgoyne. No, here he is.

BURGOYNE *enters*.

How is the Queen? Is she awake?

BURGOYNE. Awake and out of bed and asking for her nurse.

KENNEDY. Not yet, Melville. I'll say when you can see her.

She exits.

BURGOYNE. Melville!

MELVILLE. Burgoyne!

They embrace.

How is she, really?

BURGOYNE. Pretending to be strong, refusing food. But we must put some colour in her cheeks. Never let her enemies say that she was pale with the fear of death.

MELVILLE. May I see her?

BURGOYNE. She'll come when she's ready.

Two women enter in black – weeping.

MELVILLE. Sh! She's coming.

Enter MARY *– in white, wearing a necklace, a rosary on her belt. A crucifix in her hands, a crown of jewels, a black veil, thrown back. All start back as she enters.* MELVILLE *falls involuntarily to his knees.*

MARY. Now what's all this? Weeping and carrying on. You should be happy for me, for all my woes are nearly at an end. My chains are loosening, my prison walls are crumbling away and my soul's about to leap up and soar on angels wings, to eternal freedom – for ever and ever. Death approaches like a kind and helpful friend – a nice big cloak to cover up my shame. For however low we may sink, he restores nobility to us all. The crown's back on my head, and dignity and pride are in my soul once more . . .

What, Melville here? Please sir, please, up on your feet. This is your Queen's day of triumph. Her jubilee, not her death. And now I'm happy beyond all hope of happiness that my reputation will not be left in my enemy's hands, but that a dear friend of my own faith can be a witness to my final hour. But enough of me. Tell me how you have fared in this friendless, Godless land since last we met, since you were ripped from me. I've often thought of you and often wept.

MELVILLE. I've suffered nothing so great as the pain of having left your side and your service. Majesty, I've missed you.

MARY. Melville, my most faithful servant – let me tell you my last wishes for my friends and allies. Send my blessing to the most Christian King of France, to all his house. To my uncle the Cardinal and Henri Guise, my noble cousin. My blessings too to the Holy Father in the hope that he will bless me in return. And to the Catholic King of Spain, who was ready to save me and avenge me – they are all mentioned in my will – the poor gifts that I leave them are tokens of my love – and will, I hope, be valued for that.

To her servants.

The rest, the little that I still possess will be shared among you all. These clothes I'm wearing, they are yours as well. You – Alice, Rosamund, take my jewels, you're still young enough to take delight in such things. And you, dear Hanna, you have no time for gold or silver. I think your most precious jewel will be my memory. And this – this handkerchief which I embroidered just for you, in my darkest, loneliest hours – there are probably some tears stitched in there too. You used to dry my eyes when I was a little girl – now bind them tight with this – when my hour comes. That'll be the last service I ever ask of you.

KENNEDY. I cannot bear it.

MARY. Gather round, all of you. It's time to say one last word. Farewell. Farewell my dearest friends. Farewell to you for ever.

They exit sadly, except MELVILLE.

Melville, there's still one thing which stops my spirit soaring free to heaven.

MELVILLE. Tell me, lighten your burden. Share your troubles with a loyal friend.

MARY. I'm now poised at the brink of all eternity,
Ready to meet the highest judge of all.
But still I cannot make my peace with him,
A priest of my religion is denied me –
And I refuse to take the sacrament
From false practitioners of some false faith.
I want to die within the bosom of
The holy church of Rome. And nowhere else
For I can find salvation nowhere else
But there.

MELVILLE. Then take some comfort. Heaven hears
Your fervent wishes, hears them and embraces them,
And that is tantamount to their fulfilment.
Tyranny can only bind your hands
It leaves your heart free to commune with God
Words are nothing – nothing until faith
Breathes life into them.

MARY. That is not enough
Without some earthly symbol of that faith
To prove itself to Heaven. And that's why
God the father was made flesh in God

> The son, so we could see the mysteries
> Of Heaven but in human form. The in-
> Visible made visible in Christ
> Our saviour.
> The church has built a ladder which leads directly to Heaven.
> The catholic church, so called, because it's universal, meant
> and made for all to share. When thousands worship together a
> glowing fire can splutter into flame, and those flames can send
> our spirits soaring up to Heaven. Happy people. Lucky them, to
> meet and pray in the house of the Lord – where I'm shut out for
> all eternity.

MELVILLE. Not so, not so, put your trust in almighty God. If
faith can cause green shoots to grow from a dead staff, or
summon living waters from a rock, then it can make an altar in
your cell, or turn this cup into a holy vessel.

MARY. So, even though unannointed, you can be my priest, my
messenger of God, come to bring me peace and hear my last
confession.

MELVILLE. If love and longing can make a miracle, then God
will furnish that miracle to comfort you, your Majesty.

MARY. A friend from Heaven – you were once my servant – but
now serve God and speak His word. You used to kneel to me –
but look, it's my turn now!

MELVILLE. In the name of the Father, of the Son, of the Holy
Ghost. Queen Mary, have you looked deep within your heart,
and do you promise to confess the truth before the God of all
truth?

MARY. I do – my heart lies quite open to you – and to him.

MELVILLE. What sins lie heavy on your conscience since last
you made confession?

MARY. My heart was full of jealous hatred. And I had fantasies of
revenge. And, sinner that I was, I hoped for forgiveness from
God, but wouldn't even grant it to my enemy.

MELVILLE. Another sin lies heavy on your heart . . .

MARY. Yes. I have insulted Heaven not just with hatred but also
with the sin of lust. My vain heart was turned toward the very
man who betrayed me and abandoned me.

MELVILLE. Do you repent? And has your heart renounced that
false god?

MARY. That it has. It was the hardest struggle I have ever known. But now I've torn myself away from all temporal desire.

MELVILLE. Have you any other sins, which prey on your conscience?

MARY. An early crime, a bloody crime – long since confessed, which now returns to harrow my soul as fresh and foul as ever. I had the King, my husband, killed, and gave my hand and my heart to my seducer. There it is. I've confessed it and repented it for years – but it will always be a worm inside my heart.

MELVILLE. Do you have some other sin, as yet unconfessed and unrepented?

MARY. You now know everything which hangs upon my heart.

MELVILLE. Do you refuse to confess to God the very crime which drives you from this world; your part in Babington's bloody conspiracy? You are condemned for this on earth – but is it worth damnation for eternity?

MARY. As I've said, my confession is complete.

MELVILLE. Are you quite certain? Perhaps you never said the words; equivocated, yet wished for it in your heart. Those sort of tricks may deceive on earth but are nothing to the eye of fire which is to pierce your soul.

MARY. I have begged many Kings and many princes to free me from this my living Hell. But never have I plotted, neither in word, nor deed against my enemy the Queen Elizabeth.

MELVILLE. Are you prepared to mount the scaffold convinced of your innocence in this?

MARY. I don't deserve to die. But nonetheless I do thank God for letting me atone for all my crimes.

MELVILLE. Then go. And atone for them in death. This is a holy sacrifice – your blood will wash away the blood you shed before.

By the authority vested in me, I hereby justly absolve you of all your sins. Take this, the body, which was offered up for you. Take this, the blood which was shed for you. And just as you now conjoin yourself with God here on earth, so will you in Heaven. And there, there is no sin, nor suffering nor weeping – only joy – and there you'll be a rare transfigured spirit – an angel for all eternity. Amen.

He hears a noise, covers his head – goes to the door. MARY *remains in quiet contemplation.*

There is yet one harsh ordeal. Are you strong enough to conquer any hatred, any bitterness?

MARY. You needn't worry. Everything – my hatred and my love I offer up to God.

MELVILLE. Then prepare to face Lord Burleigh and Lord Leicester – for here they are.

Enter BURLEIGH, KENT, PAULET *and* LEICESTER *who stays to one side, his eyes cast down.* BURLEIGH *watches him, moves between him and the Queen.*

BURLEIGH. Lady Stuart. I've come to hear your last wishes.

MARY. Thank you my Lord. My will is with Paulet. I pray that it will be faithfully carried out.

PAULET. Be sure that it will.

MARY. I'd like my servants to be allowed to go unharmed to Scotland or to France, whichever they prefer.

BURLEIGH. As you wish.

MARY. And since my body may not lie in consecrated ground then allow my faithful servants to carry my heart back to France. Ah, perhaps it never really left.

BURLEIGH. Of course. And is there anything else?

MARY. Bear, if you would, a sisterly greeting to the Queen of England. Tell her I forgive her my death with all my heart – and that I bitterly regret my immoderate behaviour to her yesterday. May God keep her and guard her and bring her a happy reign.

BURLEIGH. You still refuse to see our chaplain?

MARY. Thank you, I have made my peace with God. Sir Paulet, I have caused you deep, deep pain. I know I have – please let me hope you'll not think of me with too much hate . . .

PAULET (*takes her hand*). God be with you. Go in peace.

KENNEDY *and the women rush in, horrified; followed by a* SHERIFF *with a staff – we see armed men behind.*

MARY. What is it, Hanna? Ah yes, it's time. This will be the sheriff come to lead me to my death. Time for us to part. Goodbye, goodbye.

(*To* MELVILLE.) I'd like you sir, and my nurse, to walk me to my death. Your Lordships surely will not deny me that?

BURLEIGH. I cannot allow it.

MARY. What? Not allow me such a tiny thing? Consider my sex, who but a woman should attend me? Not men's rough hands, I beg you.

BURLEIGH. I'll have no women on my scaffold, weeping and wailing . . .

MARY. There'll be no weeping nor wailing. Not from my faithful Hanna Kennedy. Please my Lord – don't separate me from my nurse – not now. She took me in her arms and bore me into this world, should she not lead me, gently, out of it?

PAULET (*to* BURLEIGH). Let it be so . . .

BURLEIGH. Very well then.

MARY. Now I have nothing left on earth.

(*To her crucifix.*) My redeemer, be as you are now, welcoming me to Heaven with wide open arms.

She turns to go – sees LEICESTER, *swoons – he catches her and takes her in his arms. She looks at him – he can't look back at her. Silence.*

Lord Leicester – you kept your promise. You swore you'd lend me your strong arm to lead me from my prison – and look, you're as good as your word.

He's devastated. She continues.

And I'm sure you know I wasn't only hoping you would bring me freedom – I was hoping that your love would bless that freedom and glorify my new life with you. And now I'm about to walk out of this life and into the next, I can confess without even a hint of a blush, my weakness, for now I've conquered it completely – and so, fare you well – and if you can, be happy. You dared to woo two Queens – you spurned a tender loving heart, and betrayed it, in favour of a proud one. So go and kneel to Queen Elizabeth. I hope that your reward won't prove your punishment. Farewell. There's nothing now to keep me here on earth.

She exits – MELVILLE *and* KENNEDY *at her side.* BURLEIGH *and* PAULET *follow. Others exeunt, weeping when she's gone.* LEICESTER *is left alone.*

LEICESTER. Leaving me alive. Forcing me to live. Why doesn't the ground open up and swallow me – villain that I am? What have I lost here? A pearl. The joy of Heaven. All frittered away. She has gone – her soul quite transfigured – and I'm left here, damned to despair. Where's my resolution now? I came here to muffle up my heart – to cauterise my feelings by watching her die on the block. But she looked at me, and roused up all my shame, which I thought had died. And is she, in her death, going to tangle up my heart with love? Love? Happiness? Not for you! Not any more. Batten up your heart with iron bars, be a rock. Why commit the crime if not for the reward? No. My pity shall be silent. My eyes must turn to stone. I have to see it through and watch her die.

He walks decisively to the door – stops dead, however.

Oh God, Oh Christ Almighty. This is living Hell. I can't. I can't watch. Too terrible. What's that? They're down there, getting ready, beneath my very feet. I hear their voices. Muttering, jeering. I've got to get away, got to get out. Nothing but death here, fear and death.

He tries another door, it's locked. He returns.

What's this? Is some demon forcing me to hear the things I dare not see? The chaplain's voice, exhorting her – she's interrupting him, praying out loud – listen – her strong voice. Now silence. Total silence. Sobbing now, women's weeping. They're undressing her now – removing her footstool – forcing her to her knees. And now – God – she's laying – her – head – on -

He is shaken with convulsions – appears to faint. We hear a hum of voices from below, getting louder and louder.

Act Five Part Two

ELIZABETH's *apartment as the previous act.* ELIZABETH *enters uneasily.*

ELIZABETH. No-one here yet? Not a word. Is evening never going to come? Has the sun got stuck in the sky? I can't bear to wait any longer – it's torture. Has it happened yet? Or not? I don't dare ask – both of these appal me. No sign of Lord

Leicester, nor of Burleigh. I appointed them to carry out the sentence. Where are they? Who's there?

Enter a PAGE.

So. Where are their Lordships? Well, what's the answer?

PAGE. My Lord Leicester and Lord Burleigh . . .

ELIZABETH. Yes. Where are they?

PAGE. Not here in London.

ELIZABETH. Where then?

PAGE. Nobody could tell me. They left the city in secret early this morning.

ELIZABETH (*joyfully*). Then I am Queen of England! At last I've got room to breath. But why am I shaking? What have I to fear? Surely nothing. My fear died with her – and who'd dare to accuse me? No-one. Oh no, I'll weep enough tears for her. Still here? Send my secretary Davison to me.

Exit PAGE, *enter* TALBOT.

Welcome my Lord – what brings you here so late? Something very serious, I fear.

TALBOT. Yes indeed, your Majesty, deadly serious. The doubts still lingering in my heart, coupled with my concern for your Majesty's good name, led me this morning to the Tower of London, where Mary's clerks are still imprisoned. I merely wished, you understand, to double-check their testimony. One of them, Kurl, begged me to tell him of Queen Mary's fate. For somehow they'd got wind of a rumour that she'd been condemned to death. I said she had – and in some measure, on his testimony. He jumped up like a madman and attacked his cell mate and tried to throttle him. We separated them only just in time. He then struck his breast, and cursing himself and his accomplice – wished they could both rot in Hell. He has born false witness, so it seems, and the letter sent to Babington which he had sworn was genuine, was anything but. He had tampered with the contents, writing different words from those the Queen dictated – and he was put to it, he claimed, by his comrade.

He cried that he was Queen Mary's secretary, that he was the villain who'd wrongly accused her – that he was an accursed liar and a perjurer.

ELIZABETH. Well, the man is plainly mad. And the ravings of a madman won't prove anything.

TALBOT. Your majesty, I beg you, do nothing hasty yet. Have the inquiry re-opened.

ELIZABETH. As you wish. To set your mind at rest – I'll have it done. Although I hardly think that all the peers of the realm in proper session can be described as over-hasty. But even so . . . and thank God there's still time, eh? I wouldn't want the slightest hint of doubt to taint the honour of the crown in this affair.

Enter DAVISON.

Ah, Davison. That warrant I gave you. Do you have it with you?

DAVISON. A warrant?

ELIZABETH. Yes, you remember. Yesterday I left it in your care.

DAVISON. In my care?

ELIZABETH. Now think back. The people forced me to sign it – so I signed it – under duress, obviously – so I gave it to you to keep, to kill a little time. You remember what I told you then? Well, give it to me now.

TALBOT. Do please. Things are different now. We're going to re-open the investigation.

ELIZABETH. Look, we're rather pressed for time. Where's the warrant?

DAVISON. I'm done for. I am a dead man.

ELIZABETH. Now I sincerely hope you haven't . . .

DAVISON. I am lost. I don't have it anymore.

ELIZABETH. What? WHAT??

TALBOT. God preserve us all.

DAVISON. Lord Burleigh has it. He took it yesterday.

ELIZABETH. You wretch. Is this how you obey me? Did I not command you to keep it safe?

DAVISON. Not exactly, your Majesty.

ELIZABETH. And now you accuse me of lying? Did I tell you to give it to Lord Burleigh?

DAVISON. Not in so many words, but . . .

ELIZABETH. What? You presumed to interpret my commands? If anything untoward should come of this – then by Heaven you'll pay for it with your head. Lord Talbot – you see how my subjects misappropriate my name?

TALBOT. I see it all too well.

ELIZABETH. What do you say?

TALBOT. If this man presumed to act at his own risk and without your prior knowledge, then he must stand trial before his peers, for otherwise he will besmirch your royal name, and that for all eternity.

Enter BURLEIGH.

BURLEIGH (*kneels to* ELIZABETH). Long life to your radiant Majesty – and may all the enemies of your Kingdom come to the same end as this Stuart.

TALBOT *hides his head in his hands.* DAVISON *wrings his hands in despair.*

ELIZABETH. Tell me, my Lord, did you receive the order of execution directly from me?

BURLEIGH. Not from you, your Highness, from Davison.

ELIZABETH. And did Davison deliver it in my name?

BURLEIGH. He did not.

ELIZABETH. Yet you presumed to carry it out in most unseemly haste, without inquiring if it was indeed my will? The sentence was quite just, of course, and we are beyond the world's reproach in this. Yet it was not your place to obviate the possibility of our mercy – and for this audacity you are banished from our presence – and forever.

(*To* DAVISON.) And as for you, who criminally betrayed our trust, the punishment will be the more severe. Take him to the Tower, and there put him on trial for his life. Noble Talbot. Most honest and true of all my counsellors. Henceforward, be my conscience and my friend.

TALBOT. Your Majesty. It is not prudent to banish your dearest friends, nor should you imprison those whose one desire is to serve you – and whose silence now protects you. I've served, I trust, with honour, for twelve long years. Allow me now to return the royal seal.

ELIZABETH. No, my Lord. You can't desert me now. Not now.

TALBOT. Forgive me, Majesty, but I'm too old. And this right hand has grown too old to set my seal on all your latest acts.

ELIZABETH. You'll forsake me now, will you. Having saved my life?

TALBOT. That was as nothing. If only I could have saved your honour. Long life to you, a long and happy reign. Your enemy is dead – there's nothing more to fear – and nothing left to stand in your way.

Exit.

ELIZABETH (*to* KENT, *who has just entered*). Send for the Earl of Leicester.

KENT. His Lordship desires to be excused. He has just set sail for France.

She stands motionless, trying to master her emotions.

Curtain.